Dr. Alice Says:

Healthy Horses Seldom BURP!

Other books by Don Blazer

The Match
Natural Western Riding
Make Money With Horses
Training the Western Show Horse
Nine Secrets of Perfect Horsemanship
Horses Don't Care About Women's Lib

Dr. Alice Says:

Healthy Horses Seldom BURP!

Don Blazer

All veterinary advice and opinions are those of
Dr. Alice M. Blazer

First Edition

Editor, Meribah Small

Cover art and design by Danny Elder

Success Is Easy, Cave Creek, Arizona
www.horsebooks.net

Published by: **Success Is Easy**
29025 N. 42nd St.
Cave Creek, AZ 85331

First published as a Success Is Easy paperback 1999

Library of Congress Catalog Card Number 98-91055

ISBN 0-9660127-2-0

Printed in the United States of America

When Dr. Alice was a little girl, she was crazy in love with horses. Now that Dr. Alice is a big girl, she's still crazy in love with horses.

When Dr. Alice was a little girl, she chased barrels, rode cutters and western pleasure horses, and took long trail rides. Now that Dr. Alice is a big girl, she still rides western horses, dressage horses, and sometimes takes short trail rides.

Dr. Alice has wanted to doctor horses for as long as she can recall. So she got a Bachelor of Science degree from University of California at Davis along with the 'highest honors' and the university medal for the highest scholarship.

Dr. Alice was granted her doctorate in veterinary medicine from UCD with highest honors, being first in her class, and was awarded the School of Veterinary medicine medal.

Sticking horses with western needles is good medicine, but being able to also stick them with eastern needles makes medicine even better. So Dr. Alice became certified in veterinary acupuncture by the International Veterinary Acupuncture Society.

With all those needles, a stethoscope, x-ray machines, floats, hoof testers, and bottles of pills, tablets and capsules, when Dr. Alice arrives in the pasture, horses get better. (Dr. Alice is Alice M. Blazer. Yes, she does occasionally stick a needle in husband Don Blazer.)

Whatever horsemen do with horses, Don Blazer has probably done.

With the help and guidance of an excellent horsewoman, he learned as a teenager to ride and handle most horses.

And by time he was 21, he was a professional "hoss trader." Since then he has ridden and trained Thoroughbreds to mustangs, including both western and English pleasure horses, reining horses, endurance racers and 300-yard sprinters. He has cut cattle, jumped horses, been over obstacles and around barrels.

His training philosophy is the direct result of having worked with and written about some of the greatest trainers of our time. He has taught training and horsemanship at four colleges, and he has traveled the world demonstrating training techniques at seminars and workshops. He continues to teach, lecture and participate in how-to training clinics. He still starts young performance horses, shoes his own stock and races horses at Turf Paradise.

Horses trained by Don Blazer have been to the Quarter Horse World Championships, have won at jumping, dressage and reining, as well as winning Quarter Horse and Thoroughbred stakes races.

Much of his time today is devoted to his nationally syndicated column, A Horse, Of Course, which appears in both equine publications and general circulation newspapers. He lives in Cave Creek, Arizona.

Table of Contents

4. DOES HE LOOK HUNGRY?

5. WHAT'S NORMAL?

6. NOT UP HIS NOSE WITH A RUBBER HOSE

PREFACE

It's crazy, the way we horse owners behave with our horses.

No doubt it's a love affair. A love affair of the heart, but not often a love affair in the mind. But then, seldom does a love affair have anything to do with rational thinking. Love affairs are crazy.

And what is crazy?

Crazy is mentally-unbalanced, deranged, foolish, wild or fantastic.

That's the description of a horse owner if ever I saw one.

I guess what I'm saying is we often act crazy because we act with the heart without thinking about our actions. Our intentions are good, but you know what road is paved with good intentions.

Thoughts and actions we consider rational are certainly not the thoughts of our horses, and often not what they respond to as rational.

First of all, we reason and our horses don't. We consider and make judgments as to whether or not a thing is good or bad. Our horses instinctively know what is good and what is bad. (Eating grains and tasty roughage is good--being eaten by a predator is bad. Being comfortable is good. Being jerked, spurred and worked like crazy for 20 minutes, then put away for three weeks is bad. And so on and so on.)

When do we start being crazy about horses? When we first fall in love with them. (A very easy thing to do.) And from then on, the craziness increases, almost as rapidly as the number of horses we have.

We are, almost everyone of us, crazy when we negotiate to buy a horse. A horse, I understand, is worth what someone will pay. It is impossible to establish a price when it comes to a crazy love affair. But no matter how much in love we are with the horse we want, we still have to haggle about the price. We want the price reduced, slashed, cut. It doesn't really matter how much, only that we get it down.

The price of the horse, as you already know, is the smallest amount you are going to spend. You are going to spend more for feed, more for equipment, more for shoeing and training and more for veterinary care over the next few years.

So what's the big deal about $100 or $500 or $50,000 more for the horse? Since you know a horse is worth what someone will pay for him, your horse is worth less if you get the price down.

If you love the horse, it's kind of silly to haggle over the price. Buy him.

From that moment on it's going to get crazy.

Horse owners don't know much about what they feed their horses. They usually don't have the slightest idea how many megacalories of digestible energy per day their horse is getting. If you really love that horse, then a few hours of study on nutrition shouldn't be out of the question.

But for most horse owners, buying supplements, treats, coat conditioners and energy boosters is the action of choice. Now that's crazy.

What about bits and saddles and leg wraps and spurs? What about leg cues and weight shifts and direct and indirect reins?

It's crazy to buy all that equipment, put it in and on the horse and not know how it works, why it works or if it works. But that's the standard situation. (Ask your own trainer to define a snaffle bit, and if you are told, "It has a jointed mouthpiece," find a new trainer--that one doesn't know equipment.)

Shoeing is crazy. We all talk as if shoeing were a good thing for the horse. For most horses, shoes are a means of protecting the hoof to some degree. But the instant you put a shoe on a horse, it is all downhill in regard to hoof health. And too many owners leave shoeing to the horseshoer. That's crazy! The responsibility lies with the horse's owner. Know what good shoeing is and demand it.

Veterinary care is necessary--at times.

But it's crazy to delegate your horse's health to a veterinarian. It's your responsibility to make every effort to understand your horse's needs and how to keep him healthy. When you need a veterinarian, then you need one. Most of the time you don't need one, and that's not crazy.

Am I crazy, or just in love with horses and the idea that anyone in love with a horse or horses ought to make a commitment?

Is it crazy to spend 12 to 16 hours a day working with horses, 365 days a year? Is it crazy to spend a rare day off at a horse sale, horse show or the horse races?

Boy, am I lucky to be so crazy!

And you are too, and that is why this book was written.

It's a crazy little book. It looks at horses from a different point of view.

First of all, learning about horses ought to be fun and easy and interesting and applicable.

And second, we all ought to understand that learning about horses is never ending and never complete.

This book isn't complete, but it may help you get through some of the wild and foolish years of owning horses. And it is a handy reference.

I hope you'll find this book a lot like owning horses: educational and enjoyable, never stuffy, too serious or pompous. Always a little crazy!

1

SO YOU'VE GOT ONE

So you've got a large, solid-hoofed quadruped domesticated since prehistoric times and employed as a beast of draft and burden, or for carrying a rider.

You've got an *Equus caballus*.

You've got one of those things for which there are no fewer than 132 registries in the United States.

You've got companionship, hardship, joy, frustration, relaxation, hard work, an investment and bills, and a lot of arguments as to what you've got.

You've got a horse. I'm pretty sure of that.

I'm also pretty sure I'm being politically incorrect to say it's pretty hard to tell what kind of horse you got.

First, virtually all of the 132 breed associations claim to be the association of the "most versatile horse in the world." Does that mean they are all the associations of horses with no single outstanding quality?

Second, you can't go by conformation standards as defined by the associations because, for the most part, they are all worded the same. (Does that mean a good horse is a good horse and essentially there is no conformational difference between one good horse and another good horse?)

Third, there's not much "purity of blood" when you consider there are no fewer than 35 associations for part-blood or breed by performance or breed by color.

There's an American Indian Horse Registry. That's logical. But I don't know what an American Indian Horse is, since the American Indians didn't have horses until the Spanish brought theirs in the 1500s and the Indians stole a lot of them in the 1600s. Maybe you can only have an American Indian Horse if you are an American Indian.

There are also American Mustangs. It's easier to spot an original Ford Mustang than it is to spot an American Mustang.

There are lots of color registries. Some of them make sense, such as Palomino, American Creme or American White or Paint or Pinto or Appaloosa. But what the heck is an International Colored Appaloosa? Is that a colorful Appaloosa whose color is more colorful than the not so colorful less-colored Appaloosa? And what is a Rare Color Morgan? I thought Justin Morgan was a Thoroughbred who happened to become the foundation sire for a breed which carries his name but doesn't have anything to do with color.

But then I like some of the new breeds, such as The Blazer horse. He's supposed to be quick, agile, strong, handsome and smart. (I've always maintained the Blazers have such attributes.)

Another great new registry is the American Part-Blooded Horse. If one part is blood, what is the other part? Or how about a Tennuvian or a Walkaloosa.

Anyway, let's see if you've got anything close to the following which everyone seems to agree upon:

Your whatever has a head of average size--proportionate to the horse in total. He should have large eyes with large pupils. The eyes should be set well out to the side of the head.

The nostrils should be fairly large so the horse breathes freely. The ears should be of average size with a nice little curve in at the ends and with nice points. (Don't

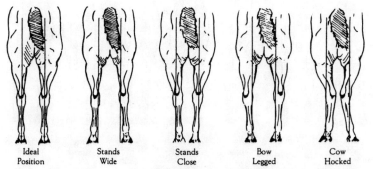

| Ideal Position | Stands Wide | Stands Close | Bow Legged | Cow Hocked |

Vertical line from point of buttock should fall in center of hock, cannon, pastern, and foot.

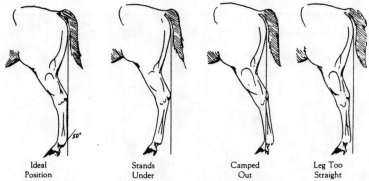

| Ideal Position | Stands Under | Camped Out | Leg Too Straight |

Vertical line from point of buttock should touch the rear edge of cannon from hock to fetlock and meet the ground behind the heel.

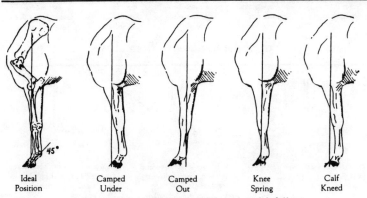

| Ideal Position | Camped Under | Camped Out | Knee Spring | Calf Kneed |

Vertical line from shoulder should fall through elbow and center of foot.

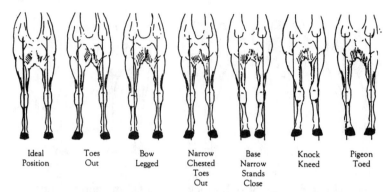

| Ideal Position | Toes Out | Bow Legged | Narrow Chested Toes Out | Base Narrow Stands Close | Knock Kneed | Pigeon Toed |

Vertical line from point of shoulder should fall in center of knee, cannon, pastern, and foot.

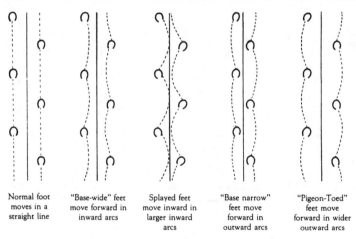

| Normal foot moves in a straight line | "Base-wide" feet move forward in inward arcs | Splayed feet move inward in larger inward arcs | "Base narrow" feet move forward in outward arcs | "Pigeon-Toed" feet move forward in wider outward arcs |

Path of the feet as seen from above

Normal foot forms even arc in flight

Too stubby — high heel and short toe causes lengthening of first half of stride, long heel touches ground earlier which shortens last half of stride.

Long toe — short heel causes shortening of first half of stride and lengthening of last half of stride.

be offended if you have burros, spotted asses, donkeys, mules, jacks or jennets, all of which have long ears, their own registries, and are *Equus asinas*.)

The horse should have a broad forehead, a well-defined jaw line, long neck, not be heavy in the crest, and have a fine throat latch.

The shoulder should slope at about 45 degrees.

A strong, well proportioned back is desirable, as is a long underline.

The hindquarters should be strong and the croup should be long and fairly level, giving good muscle over the hips. The muscle at the rear of the hindquarters should extend well down into the gaskin. The rear legs, when squared and viewed from the side, should be in a straight line from the buttock to the hock to the fetlock joint.

The hocks should be wide. They should not be too far apart, nor too close. The rear legs should be straight when viewed from behind.

Each pastern should be at just about a 45-degree angle to match the shoulder, as should each hoof.

Hoofs should be basically U-shaped, with fair depth at the rear quarter and a little more slope to the outside than the inside.

The knees should be fairly large and flat, neither being back nor over when viewed from the side. The fetlock joints should appear strong, but not overly large.

A lot of horses approximate those standards, and even if your horse does, you still can't be sure what you've got. (Take your horse into the show ring several times and you'll wonder what judges see you don't.)

When you can look at your horse without prejudice, and see his good qualities and his bad, and when you no longer care what the registries say you've got, then you've got a whole lot of something very special.

(Breed registries are listed in the appendix)

WHAT GIVES HIM THE POWER?

When you're young you think muscles are for flexing. You like to show them off. When you are older, you know muscles are for harboring aches and pains.

Actually the muscles of all animals have the specific purpose of producing motion, and in horses that includes running, jumping, bucking and kicking. Colts love to get out and exercise their muscles by zipping around the pasture, rearing, dodging and nipping at their mothers, then dashing off to join in more foal-time games. (Of course, it's nature's way of building strong necessary muscles.) Older horses, just like me, aren't so interested in exertion perceived as useless.

Muscles account for nearly 50 per cent of the total body weight of a horse. Basically, the horse's muscle system resembles that of a man in that it is directed by nerve stimulation and has the ability to contract and change shape.

There are three types of muscles. Voluntary muscles: most often attached to the bony lever areas of the horse's skeleton, they cause movement by direct command from the horse's brain.

Involuntary muscles: work without conscious direction of the brain. Involuntary muscles include those which digest food, contract the pupils of the eye or function in breathing.

Finally, there is the cardiac, or heart muscle which is in a class by itself, even though it is an involuntary muscle. A horse is said to have "great heart" when he is a champion at any performance event. And it is true that champion horses actually have larger hearts than average horses.

Most voluntary muscles are in sets of two and act in direct opposition to one anther. One muscle may be

SKELETON OF HORSE

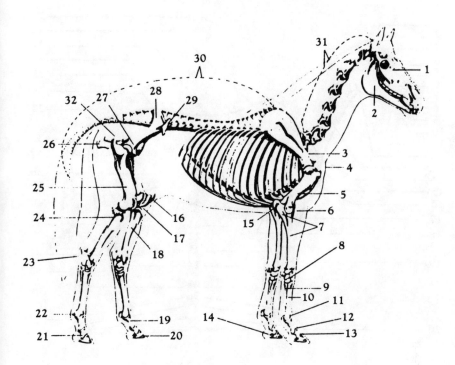

1. SKULL	16. PATELLA (knee cap)
2. MANDIBLE	17. STIFLE JOINT
3. SCAPULA (shoulder blade)	18. TIBIA
4. SHOULDER JOINT	19. LONG PASTERN BONE
5. HUMERUS (arm)	20. COFFIN BONE
6. ELBOW JOINT	21. SHORT PASTERN BONE
7. RADIUS AND ULNA (forearm)	22. PROXIMAL SESAMOID BONES
8. CARPAL JOINT (knee)	23. TARSAL JOINT (hock)
9. 4th METACARPAL	24. FIBULA
(outside splint bone)	25. FEMUR (thigh)
10. 3rd METACARPAL	26. POINT OF BUTTOCK
(cannon bone)	27. PELVIS
11. FETLOCK JOINT	28. POINT OF CROUP
12. PASTERN JOINT	29. POINT OF HIP
13. COFFIN JOINT	30. SPINOUS PROCESS
14. NAVICULAR BONE	31. VERTEBRAE OF NECK
15. POINT OF ELBOW	32. HIP JOINT

PARTS OF THE HORSE

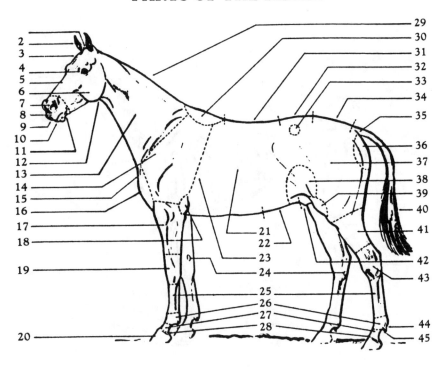

1. POLL	16. CHEST	31. BACK
2. EAR	17. FOREARM	32. LOIN
3. FOREHEAD	18. ELBOW	33. POINT OF HIP
4. EYE	19. KNEE	34. RUMP OR CROUP
5. FACE	20. HOOF	35. DOCK
6. CHEEK	21. BARREL	36. BUTTOCK
7. NOSTRIL	22. ABDOMEN	37. THIGH
8. MUZZLE	23. HEART GIRTH	38. FLANK
9. UPPER LIP	24. CHESTNUT	39. STIFLE
10. LOWER LIP	25. CANNON	40. TAIL
11. CHIN GROOVE	26. FETLOCK JOINT	41. GASKIN OR
12. THROATLATCH	27. PASTERN	SECOND THIGH
13. NECK	28. CORONET	42. SHEATH
14. SHOULDER	29. CREST	43. HOCK
15. POINT OF	30. WITHERS	44. FETLOCK
SHOULDER		45. ERGOT

contracting or flexing while the other's effort is employed in straightening or holding.

Voluntary muscles, even with good conditioning, can only work for short periods of time before they become fatigued and require rest. You will note that a horse at work will soon begin to drop his head and neck, the first sign that muscle fatigue has started. It is not long after the head and neck are lowered that the whole muscle system needs a rest. If the rest is not offered, there very likely will be some muscle damage.

Today, one of the nicest things you can do for your working horse is give him or her a good massage. (In the old days, we called it a "good rub down", and it was done after every training or performance session.) Too often the horse goes back in the stall or paddock without much attention to his tired and aching muscles. Muscle massage therapy is a good complementary health care option for the working horse.

Involuntary muscles can work for hours without showing fatigue. The heart, or cardiac muscle, gains its required rest during the split-second interval between beats.

With horses, the muscle system most subject to injury are the tendons and ligaments of the legs.

Tendons are long narrow extensions of bulky muscle. Tendons serve the purpose of taking the action of bulky muscle across joints and in changes of direction. Tendons run across the horse's knee, for example, where the bulky muscle of the forearm would not fit nicely.

Ligaments are inelastic, and primarily serve the function of holding joints in place. Ligaments around the fetlock joint, for example, allow the fetlock joint to have direct flexion, but prevent lateral or sideways movement.

Tendons and ligaments are frequently stretched,

strained or torn away from the bone when the horse is overworked and tired, or when he twists in an unnatural movement.

Short, heavy muscle denotes quickness and power, and is known as "fast twitch" muscle. It is great for a short burst of speed, but it burns a lot of oxygen and produces high amounts of waste, therefore it is only useful for only brief periods.

Longer, thin muscle, called "slow twitch" muscle, is much better for endurance, but doesn't produce the quick power of heavy muscle.

A good combination of the two types of muscle produces a well-balanced and very versatile athletic horse.

Acupuncture is being used much more frequently these days by trainers seeking to prevent muscle problems, and help heal damaged muscle without the use of drug therapy.

There is no secret to the building and caring for the muscles of a horse. Adequate rest and a good rub down (massage) help muscles feel good and regain health and strength.

Planned stresses (a solid training program) and a good diet build the needed muscle for the desired performance. And remember, horses stay fit naturally and don't need as much work as humans.

Working your horse in a designed training program is similar to sending your horse to the body building gym.

My horse can't hold a barbell, so I just let him carry a dumbbell.

WHAT'S HE GOOD FOR?

Horses are good for a lot of things. They are good to pet, and feed, and brush, and blanket. But when you get right down to the nitty-gritty, they're best for "movin'."

When mankind first met the horse he thought the horse was best for "eatin'." But he soon discovered everytime he tried to catch a bite, the horse was best for "movin'."

Horses and mankind have been doin' a lot of movin' together for the past 5,000 years, and yet, amazingly few horsemen actually know how a horse moves. Sure, sure, sure, he puts one foot in front of the other and off he goes. Sure, sure, sure, the muscles move the bones, but what we need to know is how them bones gonna move and where.

The majority of people who own horses cannot tell you the sequence of footfall for the walk, jog or lope, or the walk, trot or canter. There is a difference, you know, between the jog and trot and the lope and canter, and the difference isn't in the kind of saddle on the horse's back. The jog and lope are western gaits, in which the flight of the foot travels a more rounded arc and the horse covers less ground, essentially moving forward more slowly. Both the jog and lope are unnatural gaits and must be learned by the horse. (The western horseman wants a slow-moving horse when pushing cattle so he doesn't run all the fat off the cow and all the money out of the bank.) The flight of the foot during the trot and canter is much more natural and follows a longer, lower path. (The English rider doesn't care about fat cows, he just wants to catch the quick brown fox.)

Even though horsemen have watched horses walk for years, most don't seem to know how the horse does it. The most common error is thinking the horse begins walking by moving a front foot. He does not.

All of a horse's action initiates in the hindquarters. (That is one of the elements of training. See my book, Nine Secrets of Perfect Horsemanship.) The hindquarters push the horse forward, the horse loses his balance and reaches forward with a front leg to catch himself and reestablish his equilibrium.

The sequence of strides at the four-beat walk might be left hind, left fore, right hind, right fore. The front foot begins moving before the hind foot strikes the ground in its new position because a good horse over strides his front foot print with his hind foot. If the horse doesn't overstride, he is said to be short behind--a good indication he may be lame.

The trot is a two-beat diagonal movement. The action is still initiated by the hindquarters, but in this case, a front leg moves simultaneously. The horse may begin the trot by moving his right hind and left fore together, then the left hind and right fore together.

There is no overstriding, and the horse must shorten his body and elevate the flight of the hoof. The jog is essentially a very short forward movement while the trot should have good extension.

The lope or canter is a three-beat gait in which one side of the horse's body is extended (the leading side) and the other side is contracted (the pushing side.)

The sequence of strides for a left lead begins with the right hind foot which takes a short (pushing) stride. The left hind and the right fore then move together. The left hind is an extended stride while the right fore is a short stride.

The final (third) beat is the left fore which moves on a long stride.

Horses also pace, which means they move both legs on the same side at the same time. Sometimes it is natural. Mostly it is cultivated. If you have a horse which is not a pacer (Standardbred or other gaited breed) and he paces, it usually means he is hurting somewhere.

Some horses single-foot. A single-foot is a very smooth four-beat gait which could also be thought of as a very fast walk.

Gaited horses essentially walk, trot and canter, but with very exaggerated and flashy foot flight. There are some naturally gaited horses, although the excessive action seen in show competition is man-enhanced. The flashy action of most competition gaited horses is the result of painful training and shoeing techniques, not nature. It is most unfortunate for the horse and the act of a poor horsemen to choose to ignore such "soreing" practices.

It is also unfortunate when the standard reply of horsemen who don't know how a horse moves or the sequence of strides at a particular gait is, "So what?"

So the horse knows where his feet are supposed to go.

But when the rider doesn't, the horse is restricted, hindered, made to move incorrectly, is put under a strain and can be injured.

"That's what!"

WHEN HE AIN'T MOVIN' RIGHT

The more we know, the more complicated things become.

It used to be a horse was lame or he wasn't.

Not so today! Today the horse may or may not be "suitable for the purpose intended." That's the way veterinarians avoid saying a horse is lame or he isn't lame. Most of the time veterinarians don't perform soundness examinations. If the horse is having a problem, the owner, trainer, or stable hand usually tells someone, and if the problem can't be resolved, the veterinarian is called.

In some cases a veterinarian is called to do a pre-purchase examination. The pre-purchase examination has given too many veterinarians the idea they are "all-seeing" or somehow have special gifts no one else possesses.

Too many veterinarians are costing horses useful, happy lives being partners with humans interested in a long-term relationship. Too many veterinarians are failing horses in pre-purchase exams when the horse's actual problems--often not even identified--can be managed and the horse can have a productive future.

There is no veterinarian who can tell you what is going to happen with a horse in the next 15 minutes, let alone the next 15 years. The results of a pre-purchase exam should be an explanation of what has been found, and how it can be managed. After that, the veterinarian should remain quiet. The decisions should be made by the potential buyer, not the veterinarian.

Before any pre-purchase exam is scheduled, the potential buyer should identify the exact performances expected of the horse and the goals of the owner. If the buyer is not expecting much from the horse, and the price of the horse is small, then most often the cost of a pre-purchase exam is proportionately out of balance. The buyer might ask a veterinarian to check the horse's heart and run a blood panel to see if there are any major internal problems. More than that might not be worth the cost.

Very frequently a buyer will find a perfect horse for the tasks ahead, but the horse may have some soundess questions. If the soundness problems can be managed, then the main emphasis should be placed on the ability of the horse to provide the desired satisfaction. An older horse with some joint problems, for example, most likely won't pass a pre-purchase exam, but may still give a beginning show or pleasure rider years of service.

A pre-purchase examination should never have the goal of finding a perfect horse. If there ever was a completely sound and healthy horse at one moment, 15 minutes later he probably wasn't.

Any veterinarian who thinks he can see the future of a horse should be dismissed and replaced by a veterinarian who believes it is his job to see a problem, diagnose a disease and aid in the restoration of health.

A horse is generally considered lame when pain for whatever reason causes him to alter the usual weight distribution on one or more limbs, or exhibit abnormal extension or flexion of a joint during movement.

Seeing that the horse is lame (detection of lameness) can be easy, while the diagnosis of lameness (knowing where and why) is often complicated, unless evident in an open wound, an obvious swelling, heat or joint pain.

If the average horseowner detects the lameness, that is usually sufficient. The veterinarian stands by with special knowledge, techniques, equipment, drugs, herbs or tools to make the diagnosis and plan treatment.

Slight lameness, especially in the hindquarters, is often best detected when the horse is in a stall. When turning his forehand from side to side, the horse with a spavin or stringhalt will shift his weight onto one hind leg more quickly than to the other, which may be considered the unsound limb. If the lameness is in the forehand, the horse will be reluctant to shift his weight onto the affected limb.

A horse "off" in the forehand will often "point" the affected limb. It is not uncommon for a horse to have one foot slightly advanced when standing quietly; however, if the horse is sound, both front feet will assume equal weight.

If the horse is pointing, then the affected limb will be rested only on the toe, or heel, or if kept flat, will not bear weight. A horse lame in one front foot usually stands with the pastern straighter than that of the sound leg.

When examining a horse in movement, it is best to trot the horse. The trot is a diagonal two-beat gait at which only two feet are grounded at the same time, and therefore, each bears more weight than at the walk. When trotting, a horse lame in a fore or hind leg will favor the unsound limb at the expense of its sound diagonal. If lame behind, he will often also appear lame in front since he will put more weight on the opposite foreleg from the unsound hind leg.

A lame horse will use his head and neck for balance and to relieve weight on the unsound limb. He will raise his head when the lame front leg strikes the ground, bringing it more or less into normal position when the sound front leg is grounded. This is called "head-nodding lame," and it takes a severe lameness to cause it at the walk. It is much easier seen at the trot, especially if the handler has given the horse lead line freedom.

If the horse is lame behind, he will lower his head when the opposite foreleg is placed down.

If a horse is lame in both fronts or in both fronts and both backs, he will travel short and stiff and will lack freedom in placing his feet.

View the horse at the trot from behind. If the horse is off behind he will hitch up the unsound quarter in an attempt to keep weight off that side. Other signs of hind leg lameness are the dwelling on one foot longer than the other, or the higher lifting of one foot, or the dragging of a toe on the unsound foot.

When a horse is lame, check his feet. In most cases the cause of the lameness will be found there. If the direct cause is not found in the feet, the chances are still good a contributing cause is there.

A horse should be examined every day to make sure he isn't suffering some kind of problem. Unfortunately, we all fail to give that kind of care. But, no horseman should fail to apply the rule of no pain when a horse is being asked to work.

Horses are kind of like horsemen. If they are lame, they are lame, and need some fixin'.

But if it ain't broke, don't be messin' with it.

WHAT DOES ONE DO?

Television commercials show the world what the horse does best.

"Here comes the king, here comes the big number one." And here come the Budweiser Clydesdales, 32 hoofs in action, feathers floating as each shod foot strikes the ground, and the rhythm of it beats in your heart, and the sight is fantastic. The only time the picture is better is in the Christmas commercials when the Clydesdales are framed by the snowy decorated window and the wish is for a joyous holiday season.

How about the commercials for Visa's sponsorship of the Kentucky Derby, Preakness and Belmont Stakes? First a shot of hoofs dancing in place under the starting gate, then the gate bangs open and a burst of color and sleek muscle explodes forward, and finally, the beauty of Thoroughbreds straining, giving their all, as they reach and extend their strides just before the finish.

Television commercials are mini-epics which chronicle what a horse does best. He strides and glides, prances and dances, pulls and jumps and floats and flies.

He's action and grace and beauty and power; and every ounce of his being is "motion."

The horse first put his motion to work for man as a pack animal carrying baggage. Soon man had the horse pulling a travois, and then a chariot. As man improved on the design of the vehicles he wanted pulled, the horse improved too, getting bigger and stronger. (I must mention the horse, of course, does not pull, rather he pushes. In harness, the horse pushes against the collar, thus pulling the load. The misnomer that he pulls continues to cause the horse problems even today. But that is another story.)

For years and years the horse was man's number one source of power for vehicles which ranged from fancy coaches to light gigs.

Justin Morgan was one of the great pullers (actually pushers) of all time. He raced and won while pulling a sulky. And he won many weight pulling contests.

Today horses pull carts and buggies in horse shows. They pull logs in terrain unsuitable for machines. They pull drays in London and cabs in Central Park and they pull wagons and sleighs to promote beer.

Of course, man loves to ride the horse, and he loves it best when the horse moves smoothly. So some horses gait.

When the fastest means of transportation was by horseback, the most comfortable horses were those that ambled. The amble is a lateral two-beat gait the same as a pace, in which both feet on the same side move at the same time.

Today there is the Peruvian Paso, claimed to be the only 100 per cent naturally gaited horse. No devices, it is claimed, are used to make him perform his extraordinarily smooth, four-beat gait.

Other gaited horses include the Tennessee Walker, the American Saddlebred, the Paso Fino, the Racking Horse, the Standardbred and the Missouri Fox Trotter.

Of all gaits, probably the most spectacular is the rack. The rack is a very fast even gait in which each foot strikes the ground separately in quick succession. Over a straight course, a racking horse may cover a mile in 2 minutes, 20 seconds.

Once there was no longer a need to ride a horse for transportation, riding became fun, sport and art and in any of the three categories the horse might prance.

Most frequently you will see a horse prance in a parade. But many refined and controlled springy movements might also be called prancing. Such action includes the passage, which is a slow prancing-like trot, or the piaffe, which is a prancing-trot in place.

The classic art of equitation (riding) is known as Haute Ecole, or 'high school.' It is based on natural leaps and paces derived from tactics employed by ancient cavalry in combat.

Brought to its highest form by the Spanish Riding School, the Lipizzaners (a breed of horse from Central Europe) perform the Airs Above the Ground. The most difficult and highly publicized is the "capriole." To perform the capriole, the horse must leap into the air, then kick out with both hind feet and finally land on all four feet.

Jumping is exciting to watch and exciting to do. And horses do it well, although they really don't have the anatomy to jump vertically. Nonetheless, they do clear six feet with relative ease.

The greatest jump ever recorded that I know of was made by a Thoroughbred horse, Ben Bolt, who cleared 9 feet, 6 inches at the Royal Horse Show in Sydney, Australia, in 1936.

But best of all, horses run.

For man, horse racing may be the Sport of Kings. For horses, running at speed is the natural defense, and because horses have developed it so well, it might be called the Sport of Life.

Some say the greatest race horse of all time was Man O'War. Others say Secretariat, or Exterminator.

I think the greatest race horse was Hi School Reunion. I bet on him and he won and paid $80.

Yes, thanks to television much of the world has seen what horses do best. Horses move best.

Seeing it is wonderful, but the greatest thrill is to pull or prance, jump or run--to move--with them.

A HORSE OF ANOTHER COLOR

There's always been a lot of argument about the color of horses, but it's just a matter of splitting hairs.

Sometimes it's a matter of splitting hairs and saying what isn't the same is the same, according to a particular registry.

Sometimes it's a matter of knowing it's there, but not knowing what to do with it.

According to Dr. Ben K. Green, (the recognized authority on the color of horses and author of a book about color which took him 30 years to research), the color of a horse is determined by pigment patterns, not by pigment color.

To arrive at that conclusion, Dr. Green had to split a lot of hairs. He found that basically each hair shaft had the same amount and color of pigment, but each color had its own special pigment pattern, and because of that, he could tell the color of a horse with only one hair.

Dr. Green says a horse hair is hollow and that the walls of the hair are clear. There is only one pigment color within the hair, and that, he says, is amber.

"It is the pigment pattern and density which determines refraction of light, hence the shade of color to the human eye," says Dr. Green.

Dr. Green lists the following as the colors of horses: dark bay, (bays are brown with black mane and tail and black legs) mahogany bay, standard bay, blood bay, light bay, standard brown, seal brown, black, gray, dun, liver chestnut, (chestnuts are reddish brown with various colored manes and tails--flaxen to red, the same as the body color) dark chestnut, standard chestnut, bright chestnut, dusty chestnut, sorrel, buckskin, copper dun, red roan, blue roan, rose gray and grulla (mouse gray with dorsal stripe and black mane and tail and black legs).

Notice that he lists a lot of chestnut colors and he names sorrel as a separate color.

A number of breed registries register horses as sorrel, but the Jockey Club does not recognize that color in

Thoroughbreds. There are no sorrel Thoroughbreds, only chestnuts.

An American Quarter Horse can be a sorrel if he has a mane and tail the same color as his body coat. If the mane and tail are a different color than his chestnut body coat, he is a chestnut.

That's when different is the same, at least in some registries, and the same is different.

A horse can be brindled, but it can't be brindle.

At least, not yet.

Brindled means having a coat streaked or spotted with a darker color. In horses, it's rare, but it's there.

Brindle means having a brindled coat. There are no registered brindles in the horse world. That doesn't mean they aren't any. It means they aren't registered.

Brindle is kind of like having a bay horse which has had chocolate syrup poured over his withers, back and hips. The syrup runs down the horse's shoulders, sides and hind legs and makes irregular stripes. You know what the color brindle looks like in dogs; it's the same in horses.

But if you ask most horsemen they'll tell you there is no such thing as a brindled horse; it simply isn't known as a color.

If you ask breed associations you'll be told the association doesn't recognize the color. It isn't that they are color blind or that the color doesn't exist, it's just that they don't know what to do about it.

Dr. Green says the only undesirable colors of a horse intended for use are the dilute colors--palomino and claybank. Dr. Alice agrees, saying it is her experience that horses with extremely dilute color, such as cremellos and true albinos, tend to lack vigor and toughness. The lethal white (overo) gene leads to congenital malformations, Dr. Alice says.

Such comments should make a lot of palomino, claybank and white horse owners hoof stomping mad.

Dr. Green lists a lot of color variations and subtle differences. The breed associations basically call horses, bay or dark brown, black, gray or red or blue roan, chestnut, sorrel, buckskin, and grulla. Of course color breeds have their own special colors or color patterns.

Some associations today are suggesting there is little or no need to list black since it is almost impossible to prove the horse to be completely black. (By nature it would take 30 years or more of breeding and inbreeding to prove the horse was actually pure black and produced black.) Those who love black, however, claim science can prove the horse to be black with blood tests. (Is science always or ever right?)

Interestingly, Dr. Green claims you cannot predict the color of a foal. Nor, he says, has there ever been a breeding program more than 70 percent successful in producing colors the way genetic books say they should be produced. I can't argue with him, and I don't know of anyone who has come forward to prove him wrong.

Regardless of the color, there is an old saying about white feet which should tell you something about the experience horsemen have had over the years. It goes like this: "One white foot, buy him; two white feet, try him; three white feet, deny him; four white feet, shoot him." Despite the admonishment, horses with four white feet and four stockings are much admired and usually sell well.

White feet usually go with white legs.

White just around the coronet band is known as white around the coronet band. Amazing! If the white has some other color within the white the color is known as a ermine spot.

White up to and including the fetlock joint is known as a sock, while white which extends above the fetlock joint is called a stocking. Dr. Alice says white legs on horses are much more likely to suffer "scratches," an infection usually found on the back of the pastern and associated with dampness and uncleanness.

White on a horse does present problems, according to Dr. Green. He says white feet are prone to split, are softer and should be shod if the horse is used constantly. (Civilization being what it is, most horses today cannot go barefoot if they are being used even sparingly.)

Of white on the hide, he says the skin is quicker to scald from sweat and heat than is a dark color, especially when the white is on the horse's face and around the eyes. Dr. Alice points out that white markings with underlying pink skin make the horse more susceptible to sunburn and skin cancer.

White on the hide is known as a marking. A white spot on the forehead, between the eyes, is a star. A stripe is a line of white which can begin between the eyes and extend to the upper lip. White on the upper lip is called a snip. If the white is not continuous, the horse could be said to have a star, stripe and snip, or a star and snip, or a stripe and snip, or a star and stripe.

Pintos, Paints and Appaloosas have their own terms for certain patterns.

Markings also include swirls, whorls and cowlicks. These are changes in hair direction causing distinct patterns which are required to be identified and listed on breed registration papers. Most the time these patterns are found on the forehead and along the crest of the neck. They are also rather common on the chest and along the throat.

Other observations made by Dr. Green include the thought that the bay horse is the most durable, and that although cowboys brag about the dun and buckskin, you "rarely see fine breeding of a dun color."

Dr. Alice takes exception, saying "Excellent breeding programs over the years have refined most breeds to the point Dr. Green might only recognize them by color."

While the cowboy was sure it was the color which made duns and buckskins tougher, Dr. Green believes those horses simply took better care of themselves. "Those colors," he says, "belong to horses of western breeding. There is very little hot blood infused and self-preservation and survival are more instinctive."

Dr. Green has observed sorrels and chestnuts to have more action and more speed. But, he adds, they also have a more tender mouth. And the lighter shades of chestnut have weaker feet, he claims.

Dr. Alice says she has seen more severe cases of hives in chestnut horses than in other colors.

A gray's skin is exceptionally tough and can stand hard use, according to Dr. Green, while the palomino has the least durable skin.

And finally, contrary to popular belief--at least during Dr. Green's study--there are more bay and dark brown Arabians than there are gray Arabians.

Much of what this experienced veterinarian has to say about color will be argued for years to come.

From my point of view, a great horse is a great horse no matter what his color, and color has never made a great horse.

But then why should I even have an opinion about color--my name's not GREEN.

WHAT A HORSE IS NOT

So they cloned a sheep.

Lucky they didn't lose a chromosome.

The difference between Kentucky Derby and Preakness winner Silver Charm and a mule, is a single chromosome and no homologous pairs.

And in cloning terms, "That ain't much."

In scientific terms--which don't even pretend to tell you the difference between a horse and mule--the difference between a horse and a mule is simply that the horse cells have a total number of 64 chromosomes in 32 pairs that can be arranged in eight groups. The mule, however, has 63 chromosomes, not arranged in homologous (similar) pairs.

Had Silver Charm had only 62 chromosomes, in 31 pairs, arranged in six groups, he would have been a donkey, and then winning the Kentucky Derby would have really been spectacular.

Frankly, I didn't know all that myself. But Tom Constantino, at the time editor-publisher of *Mr. Longears*, official publication of the American Donkey and Mule Society, Inc., did know of such things. When he started telling me all this, I was all ears.

To understand more about the mule, the hinny, the donkey, or the burro, remember that *Equus asinus* is an ass (or, more commonly, a donkey or burro) and *Equus caballus* is a horse.

When you cross a male ass (jack) with a female horse, you get a mule. But when you cross a male horse with a female ass (jenny) you get a hinny.

The mule and the hinny supposedly cannot reproduce, although there are recorded cases of Molly mules having foals. Constantino said the exact mechanism involved in the maintenance of sterility by hybrid mammals has not yet been completely demonstrated, as undoubtedly there are many factors involved.

An interesting legend accompanies the cross that appears on the back of many donkeys and mules. It is said the donkey colt ridden into Jerusalem by Jesus Christ followed him to his crucifixion, and the sun's casting the shadow of the cross onto the donkey's back made a permanent mark, to be noted on the donkey forevermore. The cross on a donkey's back is described in written works appearing only after Christ's crucifixion.

The great work mules, so popular in America during the late 1700s and early 1800s, contributed significantly to our agricultural success. Standing as high as 17 hands, these mules were kept as riding animal and pets, as well as for pulling plows and wagons.

George Washington was the first president of the United States, and our first recorded breeder of mammoth mules. He had a great faith in the draft mule, and said on many occasions, "The mule is essential for America's future development." I don't think he was referring to politicians.

President Washington had a number of huge jacks standing at stud at Mount Vernon, but his favorite was Royal Gift, a large, black Catalan ass presented to him as a gift from the Spanish throne.

Today there is a rapidly growing interest in the breeding and using of mules for sport and recreation, and we even have sanctioned mule racing.

Mules may be missing a chromosome, and they may not be a horse, but they definitely are their own special creature.

2

CAN HIS DOGS BARK?

Some things are so true you get sick of hearing them.

Such as, "I hate to say I told you so, but I told you so."

Or, "Where there's smoke, there's fire."

The truest thing you can say about a horse is, "No hoof, no horse."

It's so true that nine times out of 10, when a horse is lame, the problem is in the hoof. And the one time it isn't, a hoof is probably a contributing cause.

A horse's hoof--if you stretch the comparison--is the same as the fingernail of a person's middle finger. Still comparing, the thumb and little finger long ago were transformed into the horse's ergot and the chestnut.

The index finger and the third finger are now splint bones.

The horse's foot has a functional configuration, is elaborate, and surprisingly, has a lot of moving parts.

The front hoof should be large and very round to be the perfect base to support the front leg, which supports the mass of the horse's body as it travels forward. The hind hoof is smaller and elongated so that it digs into the ground surface as it propels the horse forward.

As the hoof hits the ground, preferably flat, the hoof's quarters expand outward because the hoof is balanced and naturally shaped. At the same time, the digital cushion expands, pressing against the lateral cartilages, further spreading the quarters.

While this is happening, the short pastern bone presses the digital cushion against the frog, and the frog moves downward toward the ground. The frog absorbs concussion, compression and grips the ground.

When the hoof hits the ground, a direct concussive force is exerted upward through the multiple horn tubules--spring-like spirals in the hoof wall.

The hoof wall is connected to the coffin bone inside the foot by an interlocking of insensitive and sensitive laminae.

The narrow, but strong, hoof wall absorbs the upward force of concussion created when the hoof hits the ground, while the frog, digital cushion, coffin bone and laminae absorb the downward force of the horse's body weight--compressive force. Compressive force is so powerful it causes hoof bruises if the hoof is not able to expand enough to absorb the shock. Most of the bruises termed stone bruises are actually compressive force bruises.

The hoof is a dynamic, live, complicated structure which works quite well if strong, pliable, healthy and balanced.

Some common hoof problems are corns, thrush, cracks, seedy toe and gravel.

Corns are a bruising of the sole in the area of the hoof bar. Such bruising generally occurs because the sole of the hoof was not pared below the hoof wall at the "seat of corns," the sole area at the hoof heel. Sometimes corns are caused by improper fitting shoes. If the shoe is not set full, but is tied in too tight at the heel, the shoe will rest directly on the sole at the seat of corns.

Most horseman agree any performance horse should be trimmed or shod every 30 days. The hoof wall of the average horse will grow about 3/8 of an inch in 30 days, changing the arc of the hoof flight. The maximum length of time between trims or shoeing should normally never exceed six weeks.

Thrush is a bacterial infection that thrives in non-aerated environments. It is prevented by proper daily hoof cleaning.

Hoof cracks are simply cracks in the wall of the hoof and are called "quarter cracks" if they are in the area of the quarters, or "toe cracks" if they are at the toe. Cracks may begin at the coronet or at the weight-bearing edge. On occasion, they extend the entire length of the hoof wall. The most frequent cause of cracks is a loss of wall elasticity due to a lack of moisture. The healthy hoof is essentially 50 per cent liquid.

A cracked heel is a lesion just below the hair at the back of the hoof. Such cracks usually excrete pus. Scabs can form, then break and bleed.

Cracked heel is the result of unsanitary conditions. It can affect one or more hoofs, and it can spread to other horses.

If cracked heel becomes severe, the horse's entire leg can swell. Cleaning, drying and the application of both medication and bandages, plus general sanitation improvement, will usually solve the problem.

Seedy toe is a separation of the hoof wall from the sole. It is often associated with chronic laminitis.

Proper trimming and the avoidance of a long toe will usually correct the situation.

Gravel or sole abcesses are infections which gain entrance to the hoof through the bottom, particularly near or at the junction of the wall and sole. Such infections come on rapidly and generally make the horse very lame. The lameness will continue until the infection is removed. If it is a true gravel, the lameness will continue until the infection works it way upward through the hoof, eventually breaking out at the coronary band. While the term "gravel" is used, seldom is an actual piece of gravel involved.

If you've ever had tired or sore feet, you know what it is to have your "dogs barking."

For a horse, it's fourfold! When his hoofs hurt, you'll hear his dogs barking, or maybe they're not saying, "woof, woof"--maybe it's "hoof, hoof."

RULES TO STAND ON

I ask: Upon what will the future of the horse stand, if not upon the hoof?

And the answer comes back, "I was going to take care of his feet last week, but I forgot."

We too frequently neglect the horse's hoof.

To make neglect worse, we're breeding horses with feet too small for their size and weight.

We worry and brush and use supplements for the horse's coat, but seldom expend effort on the hoof. And when we do, it is often a dab of polish to cover past sins.

And we shoe too soon, often for the wrong reasons, and most of the time improperly.

Worst of all, because it's the underlying cause of the other problems, is the fact too many horseowners don't understand the horse's hoof.

The exterior parts of the hoof include the wall, the sole, the bars, the heel and the frog. The normal, healthy foot is strong, smooth and well-balanced. Front feet are larger, rounder and stronger than hind feet since they carry more of the horse's total weight, while the shape of the hind feet best suits the function of driving the horse.

Any ridges, rings, cracks or unbalanced shape should be considered unhealthy and abnormal.

The wall, or exterior surface of the hoof, is hard. It covers the highly sensitive interior parts of the foot and protects them from injury. The parts include the bones,

DIAGRAM OF THE HORSE'S HOOF

Normal Forefoot

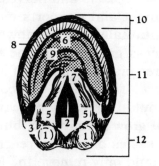

Normal Hind foot

1. BULBS
2. CENTRAL SULCUS
   OF FROG (spine/stay)
3. ANGLE OF WALL
4. BARS
5. COLLATERAL
   SULCUS

6. WHITE LINE
7. APEX OF FROG
8. WALL
9. SOLE
10. TOE
11. QUARTER
12. HEEL

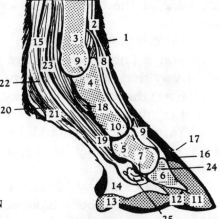

1. SKIN
2. TENDON OF COMMON
   EXTENSOR
3. METACARPAL BONE
4. FIRST PHALANX
5. SECOND PHALANX
6. COFFIN BONE
7. DISTAL SESAMOID
   BONE
8. CAPSULE OF
   FETLOCK JOINT
9. FETLOCK JOINT
10. PASTERN JOINT
11. SOLE
12. CORIUM OF SOLE
13. FROG
14. DIGITAL CUSHION
15. DEEP FLEXOR TENDON
16. CORONARY CORIUM
17. PERIOPLE
18. MIDDLE SESAMOID
    LIGAMENT
19. SUPERFICIAL SESAMOID
    LIGAMENT
20. ERGOT

21. FIBROUS TISSUE
22. SUPERFICIAL FLEXOR
    TENDON
23. INTERSESAMOID LIGAMENT
24. COFFIN JOINT
25. NAVICULAR BONE

laminae, plantar cushion, various tendons and ligaments, blood vessels and nerves. The wall has the greatest ground contact and supports most of the horse's weight. The wall continually grows down from the coronary band, and excess growth must be removed. The healthy hoof grows three-eights to one-half inch per month.

The sole of the foot is a fairly soft, shelly growth and should be slightly concave by nature. The sole and frog do not grow indefinitely, but naturally discard excessive flakes or scales once they reach their natural thickness. A shoer should only remove the loose or dead tissue of the sole and frog, never paring away live protective tissue.

The bars of the foot are actually extensions of the wall, acting as a brace to keep the foot from over expansion as weight is placed upon it.

The heel is very sensitive, with only thin wall protection and should be constantly checked for it is subject to painful ground burns or bruises.

The frog is the "V" shaped elastic substance, with its wide base at the heel and its apex near the center of the hoof.

Inside the healthy and properly-shaped hoof, the major bones and ligaments are adjusted and balanced in such a way that there are no unequal strains.

Everything is in harmony, until something gets out of balance through a lack of care or improper care.

Young horses should be trimmed regularly unless they are on extremely hard ground which naturally keeps the foot short.

A foal can have his feet rasped gently every 10 days or so to keep the foot in balance. At this early age, correct hoof balancing can help keep young growing legs straight. However, once the foal reaches the age of four months, his legs are pretty well set, and deliberately changing a natural foot angle can cause serious damage.

Don't attempt to correct legs problems by changing hoof angles.

And don't be talked into corrective shoeing. There is no such thing. There is only correct shoeing, and correct shoeing follows the rules established by nature.

Don't be to anxious to shoe the young horse. The longer he goes barefoot, the better the chance his foot will develop a naturally healthy shape, with plenty of width at the heels. The hoof is damaged with the very first shoeing and forever after needs constant attention.

Once shod, baby will need new shoes about every 30 days. The problem is not that the shoes wear out--they don't. The problem is the hoof is growing constantly, and a half inch of new growth will change the flight of the hoof in movement. Dramatic changes in hoof flight mean dramatic new stresses to ligaments, tendons and bones.

Poor shoeing of horses is very common. It is the responsibility of the horseowner to know and understand what good shoeing is, and to insist the job be done correctly. Leave the physical work of shoeing to the farrier, but final approval remains with the horse owner.

Long toes, low heels and shoes which are too small and not left wide at the quarters and heel are the greatest errors made by farriers. Don't accept such shoeing.

The angle of the hoof should not be an exact 45 degrees, as is so often quoted. The angulation should be what is natural for the horse. The proper angulation is found by keeping the hoof wall at the toe parallel with the shoulder at the crest of the withers. This angle should also have the hoof wall parallel with the long pastern bone.

An easy, close check on the properly-balanced hoof can be made by dropping a line down the center of the cannon bone. The line should touch the back of the heel at the ground surface if the hoof is to best support the horse.

The shoer should never try to straighten the horse's foot flight by changing the hoof. The hoof should strike the ground flatly no matter how crooked the leg appears to be, or how wildly it swings in flight.

Club feet are both genetic and environmentally caused.

A shoer can only help a club foot. It cannot be corrected. The problem actually is not the foot; it is the fact that the leg on that side is shorter than the other leg. The foot then grows much more straight up and down as nature's way of correcting the shortness of the leg.

The best a shoer can do is trim the club foot as nature indicates, then put a thick shoe on the foot. The normal foot should also be trimmed at nature indicates, but should have a very thin shoe applied, thereby equalizing the length of the legs.

Generally, the hoof can be rasped at the toe to reduce toe wall thickness.

The sole should be cleaned, but not pared.

The frog should be carefully maintained so it does not grow so deep there is no room for compression expansion. The frog should not hit the ground prior to the shoe striking the ground, but should grip the ground once the foot has been placed. The shoe should never be shaped to fit the foot exactly. The shoe should be left slightly wider than the hoof at the quarters and at least the width of a dime wider than the hoof at the heels.

Demand your horse wear a shoe large enough to extend beyond the hoof wall at the heel.

Finally, keep in mind the most important parts of horse shoeing are the balancing of the hoof and proper placement of the shoe to insure protection for the foot.

The least important part of horse shoeing is the horse shoe itself.

One of the greatest gifts you can give you horse is increasing your knowledge of his hoof, how it works and how it should be shod.

THRUSH IS A DIRTY BIRD

In the world of horses, thrush is not a songbird. It's a dirty bird.

Thrush is an unhealthy condition of the feet, which is most frequently blamed on dirty stalls. It ought to be blamed on horseowners.

It's true that unsanitary conditions are mainly the cause of thrush, but a lack of proper exercise can also be responsible, as can poor foot care, particularly infrequent cleaning and improper trimming of the wall, sole and frog.

The sole and frog grow only to a certain depth. Tissue which does not naturally slough away is just dead tissue which should be removed so the living sole and frog are clean.

Thrush loves to attack the neglected foot or the foot that is packed with manure and mud.

Thrush is characterized by a very offensive odor--it stinks!

And in especially bad cases, thrush produces a dark, smelly fluid similar to dirty crankcase oil. It stinks!

Thrush is caused by a bacterium, *Fusobacterium,* found everywhere, but preferring damp, wet or marshy areas. Dirty stall bedding is an ideal breeding ground.

Naturally, horses left in stalls or small corrals suffer from thrush more frequently than horses at pasture. But as the winter months approach and the rains come, pastured horses whose feet are not cared for regularly will also become victims.

If the horseman notices the offensive odor of thrush when he is cleaning the horse's feet, it's a pretty good sign additional foot care is needed.

In mild cases, thrush rarely causes lameness and is relatively easy to treat. However, in severe cases, where discharge in the crevices around the frog is evident, lameness can develop. Thrush lameness is very difficult to cure, difficult to treat and often requires the services of a veterinarian, says Dr. Alice.

Often thrush is a spin-off disease created by another lameness. If the horse has thrush in just one foot, rather than both front feet, then lameness from another source should be considered, even if it isn't yet observable.

Prevention of thrush, of course, is the best cure.

The horse's feet should be cleaned thoroughly each day. It takes only a moment or two and is not asking too much of the thoughtful or concerned owner. The horse's feet must always be cleaned before working.

If thrush develops, trim away the infected portions of the frog, and be sure to clean the crevices between the frog and sole completely, says Dr. Alice. As soon as the foot has been cleaned, you can pour a household bleach into the crevices, making sure the bleach does not slop over onto the heel or coronary band.

Dr. Alice says a tincture of iodine or a commercially produced medication designed specifically for thrush can be applied to the diseased frog.

An old-time remedy for thrush is a poultice of boiled turnips to which a few drops of carbolic acid or powdered charcoal have been added. The poultice should be kept on the foot for two or three days. (Frequent treatments with bleach are faster, easier and probably just as effective.)

Stalls, corrals or paddocks should be cleaned often and fresh bedding should be supplied regularly. Check stall drainage so pools of urine or water do not collect.

Good, consistent exercise keeps the foot healthy and is an excellent preventive measure, especially since the foot should be cleaned thoroughly before exercise.

FOUNDER IS NOT SOUNDER

When most people talk of founder, they are referring to something bad, which it is.   They think it is something caused by eating too much grain, which it can be, or something not often seen, which is wrong.

Founder is an old name. The more modern name is laminitis, which means there is an inflammation of the laminae of the foot. The inflammation may be caused by infectious or noninfectious agents.

Both the causes and the treatment of laminitis are very much under study, and there is still a great deal of disagreement about the condition.

"What we know for sure," says Dr. Alice, "is laminitis is a much more common occurance than most horsemen previously believed."

Laminitis can affect both front feet, which is common, or all four feet. If all four feet are affected, the horse will tend to lie down for extended periods. If only the front feet are affected, the horse will extend the front legs to stand pretty much on his heels in an effort to eliminate weight from the feet.

Heat is present in the sole, wall and coronary band, says Dr. Alice. The arteries that run down the pastern throb, and tapping the hoof even lightly causes pain.

The horse with laminitis suffers great distress and is unwilling to move.

Grain founder is well-known and is probably the most common cause of laminitis, says Dr. Alice. But pure and simple overfeeding creates an overweight situation which in turn is an adjunct to grain founder. With grain founder, ingestion of greater quantities of grain than can be tolerated is the cause, Dr. Alice says. Such founder is often accidental, such as a horse getting into an open grain bin. Overfeeding, again the ingestion of more feed than can be tolerated, is usually the result of a softhearted horse owner trying to make the horse happy.

A horse can founder when he drinks large amounts of cold water immediately after he has become overheated.

Horses can founder from having their feet "cook" while they ride in a trailer without sufficient floor insulation. The extreme heat of summer highways in the southwest rises from the pavement through the bottom of the trailer and into the bottom of the horse's hoofs.

Grass founder is common among horses that are grazed on summer pastures, especially if the pastures contain clover and alfalfa. When overweight horses are turned out in lush grass pastures, founder is frequently the result.

Ponies are especially susceptible to laminitis, Dr. Alice says.

Lack of sufficient exercise is another cause, which is possibly becoming much more common. Horses left in box stalls for long periods, then taken out and worked, are good candidates for laminitis. Such a founder may be similar to what was known as road founder, the result of concussion to the feet from hard or fast work on a hard surface. Horses out of condition are especially subject to such founder.

Once the horse has suffered from laminitis, there are usually heat rings around the hoof wall, and the hoof, over a period of time, tends to curl up at the toe.

Even when a horse is lucky enough to recover from a case of founder, the rings or ridges may continue to appear on the hoof wall for years. The front of the hoof wall may have a permanent dip.

In a severe case of laminitis, there is often a dropping of the sole and a rotation of the coffin bone, says Dr. Alice. Rotation, or downward point of the coffin bone, can be seen in radiographs.

In any case of laminitis, the prognosis is always guarded. If the symptoms continue for more than 10 days, the future for the horse is unfavorable, Dr. Alice warns, especially in the case of rotation of the coffin bone.

The signs of founder are quite obvious, and a veterinarian should be called *immediately.* The quicker aid is given, the better the chances of reducing the damage. Laminitis should always be considered an emergency situation, Dr. Alice emphasizes.

If your horse is showing signs of laminitis, stand the horse in cold water, call your vet, and keep the horse in the cold water until the vet arrives. It may or may not help.

Do not exercise a horse you suspect may be suffering from laminitis.

If you have reason to believe the sole has dropped or the coffin bone has rotated downward, wad up some old rags and tape them to the bottom of the foot directly over the apex of the frog. Or, Dr. Alice says, you can tape a tennis ball to the bottom of the foot or feet. The idea is to be sure there is an upward pressure against the coffin bone. Now call your veterinarian.

Depending on the type of founder, the veterinarian will formulate a treatment. (There are some pretty radical treatments these days. Be cautious about treatment choices, Dr. Alice advises.)

At the vet's direction, assistance from a horseshoer may eventually get the horse suitable for work. Frequent hoof trims, the use of a wide web shoe or leather or rubber pads, or an egg-bar shoe may be recommended. Again, be cautious in selecting shoeing remedies.

Laminitis is not a problem to be taken lightly, cautions Dr. Alice. While it isn't often fatal, but can be, it can quickly render a horse useless.

And minor cases of laminitis, Dr. Alice adds, are much more common than the average horseowner believes.

COMMONLY 'UNWANTED'

Ringbone and sidebone are two nasty conditions seen rather frequently in backyard or pleasure riding horses, but are not generally common among top show or racing stock.

Both conditions are associated with poor conformation and therefore don't appear as often in horses selected for their correctness of form or athletic abilities.

Ringbone is nothing more than degenerative arthritis with new bone growth around the joints of the first and second, or second and third phalanges. The conformation of the horse may tend to encourage a binding force on the joints of the coffin and pastern bones. A failure to keep the horse's hoofs trimmed regularly, or improper trimming with a long toe and short heel, results in stress on the front of the pastern and coffin joints. Such unrelieved pressure, or even some type of external trauma, may initiate new bone growth. Ringbone can also result from infections such as navel ill (discussed in Chapter 8) and from nutritional unbalances, Dr. Alice points out.

The new bone growth, Dr. Alice explains, is the response of damaged bone tissue.

Any lameness, whether from high (pastern joint) or low (coffin joint) ringbone, results from the irritation caused by the new bone growth.

In a few cases, there will be little or no lameness with ringbone. However, says Dr. Alice, when there is lameness, it is usually evident at any gait, but is most pronounced when the horse is trotted in a circle.

Inflammation is often involved and there can be an obvious enlargement on the front of the pastern. Ringbone can affect both front and hind feet, but is most common in front.

The treatment, says Dr. Alice, usually involves therapy to reduce the inflammation caused by the ringbone. Anti-inflammatory drug therapy and improved shoeing are used with some success.

Sidebone is an ossification of the lateral cartilage and can be inside, outside and on one or both front feet just above the coronet band.

Normally, if you press your thumb against the bulb of the heel it has a springy feeling. When sidebone is present, the area will be hard and immovable, observes Dr. Alice.

There are probably three causes of sidebone.

Trauma to the area, Dr. Alice says, is one possibility, but the least likely.

Poor conformation, especially a toe-in or toe-out, is common with sidebone.

Poor shoeing that gives the foot an improper angle or causes the foot to strike the ground unevenly is frequently a cause of sidebone, according to Dr. Alice.

With poor conformation or poor shoeing, there is an unequal stress on the foot. One result can be the ossification of the lateral cartilage.

"Rarely does sidebone cause lameness, except in the early stages of formation when there is inflammation," states Dr. Alice. "Lameness generally follows a fracture of the sidebone. In other words, an enlargement of bone is produced, then it fractures, and the broken segment moves and causes pain."

Sidebone may be effectively treated by preparing special shoes for the horse. "What must be accomplished," she adds, "is the elimination of pressure to the injured area."

If corrective shoeing isn't the answer, a neurectomy (heel nerving) may be the only solution.

"Once it has been established that sidebone is the cause of lameness, heel nerving is a viable option to the horseowner," Dr. Alice says. "I've had very good success with neurectomies. Many horses have been used for years after heel nerving, free of pain."

Both ringbone and sidebone can easily be seen in radiographs. So if you are suspicious, use the technology.

Once the radiographs have been read, the veterinarian will have a much better chance of prescribing a successful remedial program, Dr. Alice believes.

THE DISEASE THAT ISN'T

Navicular disease isn't, but what it is, is probably much more common and afflicts many more horses than most horsemen would guess.

Navicular disease is a misnomer. Actually what we have when we have an inflammation, or bruise, or adhesions between the navicular bone and the deep flexor tendon, is a "navicular condition," explains Dr. Alice.

"And a navicular condition is one of the major causes of lameness in horses," Dr. Alice affirms.

Navicular problems are not always diagnosed early, says Dr. Alice, because frequently the lameness clears up when the horse is given a bit of rest, or the lameness is thought to be in the shoulders, or, if radiographs are taken, there are no significant changes seen in the navicular bone.

The degree of lameness suffered by the horse is seldom directly related to the amount of changes seen in radiographs, Dr. Alice says. The sensitivity of the horse and the degree of damage to soft tissue (which can't be seen on radiographs) are determining factors, she said.

Dr. Alice believes one of the principal causes of navicular conditions is poor shoeing.

It has become quite common today for horse's heels to be cut quite low, and the toes to be left long. The effect is to break the pastern bones back, causing the deep flexor tendon, which runs across the navicular bone, to assume an unnatural strain.

The insidious nature of this situation, according to Dr. Alice, is that the navicular bone and the deep flexor tendon get no relief, even when the horse is standing quietly in his stall. So a navicular condition may develop over a period of time, even though the horse may appear perfectly at ease.

Dr. Alice suggests all horseowners keep an eye on stalled horses and become concerned if they make small mounds of stall bedding to help elevate their heels while they are standing. A horse working to elevate his heels is telling you he has a problem, she warns.

Navicular condition has been attributed to many causes. Some of the causes are genetic predisposition, conformation, improper shoeing, type of work performed, nutrition and the breeding of large horses with small feet.

According to Dr. Alice, horses suffering a navicular condition may demonstrate an unnatural gait. If the horse appears to be tiptoeing across eggs when at work, a trainer or rider has reason to suspect navicular condition.

During movement, the horse will tend to land on the toe of the foot to avoid concussion to the heel area. Usually, the condition is found in both front feet. The signs of lameness often shift from one front foot to the other. (Navicular lamenesses are seldom discovered in hind feet.)

Once the condition has progressed, the horse will usually show lameness after working, then get better with rest. Once put back to work, the lameness will return.

Dr. Alice believes horses with navicular condition must have their hoofs correctly balanced by trimming and shoeing and must have consistent, moderate exercise.

"I don't believe it is in the best interests of the navicular horse to prescribe stall rest.," Dr. Alice advises. "The horse will only improve with treatment and exercise."

A veterinarian can often determine a navicular condition with the aid of hoof testers which are used like pliers to apply pressure to the foot.

Radiographs will not often show significant navicular bone changes in the early stages of the condition, but a nerve block--elimination of pain--will usually aid in diagnosing a navicular condition.

According to Dr. Alice, while the prognosis is not favorable in many cases, there is a lot which can be done to help the horses.

"If caught early enough, carefully-monitored shoeing can help the horse," Dr. Alice says.

What is required, primarily, she believes, is the restoration of the hoof to its natural shape and balance. Drug therapy is used to reduce inflammation.

If the condition is severe and chronic, it is possible to salvage a number of useful years of service by performing a neurectomy (heel nerving) on the horse.

3
HE'S GOT 5 SENSES
AND
A VOCABULARY TOO!

Humans need to communicate. Horses need to communicate. And horses and humans need to communicate with each other.

Communication is the basis for all horsemanship.

Training is actually nothing more than teaching a method of communication. (Worldwide, the perfect idea would be that everyone use the same system of communication, then everyone could effectively ride every horse, and every horse would understand what was being asked.) When messages get mixed up or misunderstood, the horse doesn't react in the manner desired by the human. When the message is understood, the horse reacts as desired, and harmony exists.

So horsemanship is communication.

Everything a horse will be asked to do--walk, trot, canter, jump, spin, stop, sidepass, back, run, change leads, collect--can be done from the time he is about two hours old. No man teaches him to do it; it is his nature.

If the horse's movement is natural, then he isn't trained to perform; he performs in response to a request.

Since man is doing the asking, then man is responsible for teaching the language.

The horse is never to blame for not knowing what to do or how to do it. The trainer, rider or handler is always to blame if the horse does not understand what is being asked.

The physical conditioning of a horse is also the responsibility of man (trainer). The trainer must formulate a plan of exercise designed to make the horse physically capable of performing the work being asked without suffering injury.

The human, who is supposedly of superior intelligence (the only one arriving at that conclusion is man), always expects the horse to understand the human's message. Seldom will you ever hear a human say, "Apparently I was not clear in my request."

Why is it the one supposedly of superior intelligence always expects the one of supposedly less intelligence to do all the work of learning?

The really intelligent horseman doesn't expect the horse to learn his language without the horseman first learning the horse's language.

Researchers estimate the horse's vocabulary at 47 basic messages with 30 variations of inflections, or a total of 1,410 communicative expressions.

Ah, but the horse uses his eyes, ears, nostrils, tail, muscles and voice to deliver his messages.

A horse's nostrils quiver, expand and contract to register interest, suspicion, fear or temper.

A horse's tail is an indicator of his health or state of mind. To show elation, the tail is held nearly parallel to the spine. Exhaustion is signaled by a quivering tail and a switching tail indicates fear or pain. If the horse clamps the tail down tightly, he is being asked to approach something that terrifies him.

It is interesting to note that experts say if a stallion is used exclusively for breeding, his vocabulary is limited pretty much to enthusiastic and noisy outbursts at the sight of a mare. However, if the stallion is put to work and placed in varied situations, his vocabulary usually expands rapidly.

Experts on horse vocabulary agree a stallion used under saddle seems to have more winning ways with broodmares as a result of his enlarged vocabulary. (That apparently holds true for humans too, as the macho man may initially be exciting to women, but he generally loses to the more stable smooth talker.)

It has been proved that when a horse realizes you are trying to understand what he is saying to you, his vocabulary will increase, sometimes double. The horse will make a genuine effort to communicate with you.

The horse can tell you what he's thinking.

The best horsemen listen, teach the horse a common language, then make their requests.

And the thing that makes the partnership so wonderful is the fact the horse is such a good listener.

INSTINCTS RESULT IN BEHAVIOR

If you don't know the language, you can't communicate well.

It's the trainer's responsibility to understand how a horse thinks and why he thinks that way. When the trainer understands the horse's mental process, then the trainer will be able to develop a language the horse can understand.

Mentally, the horse is consistent and reasonable. Unfortunately for the horse, much of the time his handlers aren't reasonable. When they aren't reasonable, they lose self-control and forget it's a matter of communication.

On the other hand, most handlers are consistent--always blaming any error or misdeed on the horse.

Genuine communication is possible only through a knowledge of the horse's mental processes, which are, in order of importance: herd instinct, need for security, the following instinct, love of routine, laziness, excitability and nervousness, sensitivity and courage.

Even though most horses don't live in a herd today, it is the companionship instinct that is strongest. (Instinct, by the way, is the word science uses when science doesn't know why something is the way it is.) Young horses and horses not trained are most reluctant to leave a group, but when the training process begins, they are frequently forced to do just that, and the trouble begins.

The herd instinct, however, can be helpful, and is for the intelligent trainer. Such a trainer will see to the following: young horses are accompanied by an older, trained horse. Training areas are, by design, close enough to home (the stall or corral) to be familiar, yet are far enough away from a group of horses so as not to be distracting. Young horses are allowed to watch companions perform prior to being asked for the same exercise--such as crossing water or jumping, and horses being schooled are worked toward their friends, rather than away. Using the knowledge of the herd instinct is the first step in developing a common language.

As the horse learns to respect and trust the handler, the horse will become more secure (security) and therefore, more calm--a prerequisite to training.

The following instinct (translation--obey) is a great assistant to the trainer-rider, if put to use.

Most horses have a natural inclination to obey, which make them surprisingly cooperative. But this is a double-edged sword. If the handler knows what he is asking, and is consistent in doing so, the horse will eventually perform exercises as they were intended. If the handler doesn't know what he is asking, the horse will still eventually perform as he perceives the request, by running away, throwing his head, stopping at jumps, etc.

By dominating the horse consistently and reasonably, instead of employing cutesy, lovey nonsense, the handler is filling a basic need (the "following" instinct) in the horse, and the horse responds.

The love of routine is basic to the horse's security, calm and well-being, just as it is basic to training methods. Good trainers map out a program of progress for the horse, repeating basic steps and building upon them. The poor horseman jumps from one exercise to another, never establishing anything except frustration.

The love of routine is linked to the horse's natural laziness. Understanding that, it is foolish for a rider to ask more of a horse than is required. If a horse gets an exercise correct, and demonstrates he understands the rider's request, why keep asking the horse to do it over and over again until he is exhausted? Instead, use the love of routine the next day by repeating exercises the horse knows how to do. Everyone, including the horse, likes to do what he can do well, and he likes to be praised for his accomplishments.

Horses are also excitable and nervous, traits that in years past helped them to avoid predators. The horse's nervous system is highly tuned, and shouting at or abusing a frightened horse only makes matters worse.

Linked to excitability and nervousness is the great sensitivity of the horse, without which it would be impossible to achieve subtle cues. Knowing of the horse's sensitivity, the good trainer always begins with a minimal cue, never with a forceful one.

The most useful attribute of the horse's mind is his extraordinary memory. Put in the correct things and you get the correct response. Put in anything else and that's what you get back.

For the memory to work well, however, cause and effect, reward and punishment, must be closely related in time.   Don't wait to praise the horse when he does something well, or to punish the horse that knows better, but has refused to comply.   Take praise or disciplinary action immediately.

The horse's great courage is demonstrated by his repeated, and often thwarted, attempts to trust man.

They say it is horse sense which keeps horses from betting on humans.

I agree.

It's knowing a horse has horse-sense which keeps me betting on the horse rather than the human nine times out of 10.

EARS TO HEAR AND HOLD

He's got ears--they hear, and he talks with them, and they can tell his temperature, and at times they make a good handle.

Horses have an extremely good sense of hearing. Little is actually known about how they hear, but it is suspected his hearing is more similar to, rather than different from our hearing.

Humans hear a range of sounds from 30 to 19,000 hertz. Horses can hear a range of 55 to 33,500 hertz. So a human can hear a few lower sounds, but horses hear many more sounds through the higher frequencies.

While their hearing is very sensitive, it is not very precise.   The horse may pick up a strange sound, but since he has difficulty placing its exact location, he spooks. Spooking is actually just getting ready to "get the heck out of here just in case what I hear wants to eat me." Horses share this trait with other animals of prey.

Predators, on the other hand, can pinpoint a sound's location.

While working around a horse, keep in mind he will not hear you if you talk in a very low pitched voice. At the same time, he may hear high range sounds you don't hear, and he may spook, perceiving the noise as threatening.

The tone of voice you use tells your horse plenty. An uncertain tone allows him to ignore you and disobey. A definite and steady voice tells him you mean exactly what you say.

A lot of sounds are extremely irritating to some horses--clippers, for example. An irritating noise can actually cause a horse to lose his ability to concentrate on the performance you are requesting. For example, your horse may be perfect in the warm-up arena, but distracted by the organ music at the main show arena. Exposure to such noise, plus your calm reassuring voice, can help the horse get over the fear.

A horse talks with his ears by moving them about and telling you exactly what he is concentrating on. A horse's ears are either forward, back or sideways, but almost always active.

A horse's ear points toward whatever he is looking at. (More later about how he sees in two directions at the same time.) If both ears are pointing forward, the horse is very attentive to something he sees. If his ears are casually moving about, he is relaxed and just checking things out.

If his ears are nearly flat on his head, he has "sour" ears and dislikes his companions, his rider, or what he is being asked to do.

Be very careful around the horse which puts his ears flat back on his head. He is about to bite you, kick you, or he is telling you not to mess with his ears because they hurt.

A horse's ears are normally very cool. But when the horse is not feeling well and has a temperature, you'll be able to feel the heat in his ears.

Luckily, horses don't have a lot of problems with their ears, says Dr. Alice.

One of the most common discomforts a horse suffers is infestation by ear ticks. These parasites invade the ear canal, becoming extremely irritating. The horse will shake his head, but to no avail. He'll lay his ears back and he'll resent anyone touching the ear.

There's no way you'll be able to get the ear ticks out, so call a veterinarian, Dr. Alice adds. The vet will provide a medication to kill the ear ticks.

Wax buildup in the ear is also very uncomfortable for the horse. Ear wax can be dissolved with cerumenolytic agents, which can be provided by your veterinarian.

A lot of horses get flat, gray warts in their ears. These are persistent, but usually don't bother the horse too much. Treatment for such warts is usually not recommended, according to Dr. Alice. In most cases these warts are more troublesome to the horse's owner than they are to the horse. Sarcoids are relatively common, as are melanomas on or in the ears of gray horses.

The tips of the ears are often frozen off horses which are pastured in extremely cold areas. Foals born in the high country often lose the tips of their ears due to frostbite. The tips of the ears are generally the last part of the new foal to dry and are, therefore, susceptible to the cold.

And the ears are very subject to wounds. Split-eared horses are a pretty common sight. Such splits can usually be repaired with cosmetic surgery.

Even splits several years old can be repaired by a skilled vet, says Dr. Alice.

There are several conditions that do not involve the ear itself, but which may affect the horse's hearing.

Parotitis is swelling and inflammation of the parotid salivary gland, just below the ear. If he has parotitis, the horse won't like you fooling with his ear.

Diseases of the guttural pouch can also cause a swelling beneath the ear. The guttural pouch is peculiar to the horse. It is a sac that opens into the eustachian tube of the inner ear, Dr. Alice explains. It can become infected. Sometimes with foals, it distends with air, causing a condition known as tympanitis.

Tympanitis and parotitis both need the attention of a veterinarian.

Finally, a horse's ear makes a good handle if it is necessary to restrain a horse. A lot of people mistakenly claim "earing" a horse will make the horse ear-shy. If done properly, earing is a satisfactory method of restraint which will leave no ill effects.

Attacking a horse's ear suddenly, or trying to bully the horse by pulling the ear with extreme force, will make a horse ear-shy.

But if the ear is grasped gently, then intermittent and powerful pressure is applied with the fingertips, and the ear is released slowly, the horse will show no signs of shyness or discomfort.

GOOD LOOKERS ARE SMART

Horses have remarkable eyes.

They can, at one time or another, and sometimes in combination, have a feather in the eye, a glass eye, a pig eye, a pop eye, a smoky eye or a walleye.

In addition, they have both monocular and binocular vision. The horse uses monocular vision to view separate things with each eye at the same time. These objects are to the side and rear of the horse. Binocular vision, for the horse, is frontal vision, and for it the horse concentrates both eyes on the same object. (Remember a horse's ears point where the horse is looking, whether together or separately.)

The horse can see to the front, the side and the rear. In fact, he has a field of vision of up to 300 degrees.

But his wide-angle vision may adversely influence his ability to learn or the level of his intelligence, or both. Large eyes, set well out to the side of the head, have always been considered a mark of quality in the horse. And while the horse should have large eyes, having the eyes placed well out to the side may be a handicap for the horse--from a learning point of view.

The farther out the eyes are placed on the side of the head, the more the horse must concentrate to achieve front vision. Distractions limit his ability to concentrate, which in turn makes him slower to learn, or, as some might say, less intelligent. On learning ability scales, animals that have just frontal vision generally rate higher than animals with monocular vision.

But this is only one of the horse's vision-related limitations.

We are pretty sure the horse does not see in color. And we know the retina of the horse's eye is somewhat flattened rather than curved. This means objects are quite frequently out of focus. To bring them into focus, a horse must lower, tilt, or raise his head.

The horse's eye does not focus well on objects that are closer than four feet, and when a horse has his head high in the air, he cannot see the ground in front of him. Because of a special system within his eye, the corpus negre or black body, which absorbs light rays from above, the horse cannot see clearly that which is above the level of his eyes.

And while the horse has a wide field of vision, he does have two blind spots. They are close to his face, directly in front of him and the width of his body directly behind him. These blind spots are the cause of many problems for both horse and man.

All the special advantages and limitations of the horse's vision have a great deal to do with the way the horse behaves.

Just imagine what a young horse sees the first time he is taken on a trail ride or to a horse show!

There is the excitement of a strange place, cars, motorcycles, people, noises and all sorts of unknown objects. Moreover, at any time there is always something happening on each side of the horse. In many cases, the action isn't in focus, and even if it were, the horse wouldn't understand it. To see what is going on in front of him, the horse must concentrate his full attention straight ahead, but how can he do that when there is so much new and interesting to see on each side of him?

Seeing is certainly disbelieving for the young horse. He must be asking himself, "How could my master put me in such an incomprehensible world?"

Can you blame him for being a little flighty?

Most of us do, and consequently try to jerk, spank or force the horse into being calm when he is upset.

Such action will not work. Only understanding how the horse sees will help.

With all that seeing going on, get a look at the terminology, such as "feather in his eye." A feather refers to a visible blemish on the eye. The blemish may be the result of an injury or a natural defect. In either case, it is considered a fault.

A glass eye lacks color and may be the cause for disqualification by some breed registries. A pig eye is a small squinty eye, and a horse that has pig eyes is generally considered stubborn and hard to handle.

A pop eye is the opposite of pig eye; it is the description given to an eye that seems to be too large and protruding from the head.

A smoky eye is an eye that is cloudy in color, almost smoke gray.

A walleye is another term for an eye without color and is sometimes referred to as a China eye.

SKIN DEEP

He feels the softest of caresses.

He feels the pressure of the lower leg.

He feels the sting of a whip.

He also feels the discomfort of an itch, a sunburn and a variety of rashes, as well as the irritation of a fly, a tick or the bite of an ant.

All this feeling a horse does with his skin--a part of him we seldom see.

We see the glossy sleekness of a velvety coat, but we don't often see the superficial non vascular (without blood vessels) layer, the cuticle or epidermis. And unless we are looking at a major wound, we never see the deep vascular (with blood vessels) layer, the corium, dermis or true skin.

And we practically never think of the fact there is an intimate nervous sympathy of different points of the skin with particular internal organs.

In the horse, as well as in man, certain skin disorders can be caused by internal disease, and certain internal diseases can cause various skin problems, says Dr. Alice.

A skin eruption often follows certain disorders of the stomach, the liver, the kidneys or even the lungs. A simple burn of the skin can cause inflammations of internal organs, and inflammation of such organs can, in their turn, cause eruptions on the skin, Dr. Alice explains.

It is a good idea to view skin problems as a signal there may be other health concerns to consider.

A visible disorder in the skin of a horse may point of a particular fault in diet, to an injudicious use of cold water when the horse was overheated, to a fault in the stable's drainage, ventilation or lighting, she points out. It is worth giving full consideration to such possible causes before jumping to the often erroneous, but common, conclusion that when a horse is suffering from strange lumps or bumps on his skin, they are mosquito bites.

Of course, they could be parasitic skin diseases caused by flies, leeches, lice, ticks, poultry mites, mange or ringworm (commonly known as "girth itch.")

On the other hand, it could be simple eczema.

Or it could be an allergic reaction to fly sprays, the use of certain drugs or a fungus.

Dr. Alice says skin problems caused by allergies can also be accompanied by swelling around the eyes, swelling of head and legs, labored breathing, an increased heart rate and sometimes a sticky serum on the skin.

The best treatment for an allergy is, of course, the removal of the thing to which the horse is allergic. If you can't determine the cause of the external skin reaction, then give the horse a little time and he'll probably build up an immunity and the lumps or bumps will go away, she says.

However, if the horse is in discomfort, and the allergy symptoms are pronounced, call your veterinarian. The vet may not know the cause, but can at least treat the symptoms, providing immediate relief from the pain or itch.

Biting flies cause a horse a lot of skin problems. Many horses are so sensitive to fly bites, especially on their legs, they suffer from scabby sores and bleeding.

The best method I've found for eliminating this problem is to have the horse wear socks during the worst of the fly season. A pair of athletic socks, with the toes cut out, slip easily over the horse's leg and with a tiny bit of masking tape, stay in place nicely.

Horses with a lot of white on their heads, especially around the eyes and muzzle, are subject to severe sunburn. A little dab of zinc oxide ointment will help relieve the pain and prevent further burning. The most effective prevention technique is to keep the horse from playing too long around the pool or on the beach.

Some horses are pretty thick-skinned, and it really doesn't matter what you say about them. They ignore all derogatory comments. Others are a little thin-skinned, and you have to be careful what you say, or you might hurt their feelings.

In either case, you must remember, beauty is only skin deep, so take care of your horse's skin.

You know how vain he is!

OPEN WIDE

I don't think the majority of horses like the dentist any more than I do.

But just the same, they need regular checkups--at least twice a year.

Even though they don't brush after every meal, they seldom have a cavity--just a few rough edges.

The rough edges develop because the horse's upper jaw is wider than the lower jaw. Therefore, the outside edge of the upper molars and the inside edge of the lower molars are not worn smooth during the grinding process of chewing. These sharp edges can cut the inside of the horse's mouth and make him most uncomfortable.

To smooth out the situation, and get the horse chewing properly again, the veterinarian will "float" the horse's teeth. Water isn't used to do the job--a long-handled rasp, known as a "float," is used.

Horses frequently object to having their teeth filed, but not because it hurts. They don't have the same type of nerve system as humans, Dr. Alice explains. The filing doesn't offend them. It's the gigantic steel toothbrush they dislike. Dr. Alice says the teeth of young horses are relatively soft, and need to be floated more often than the harder teeth of an older horse.

Horses aren't crazy about having their teeth pulled either. Again, it isn't that it hurts. The horse just figures it's easier if he spits them out when he's ready. (If for some medical or trauma reason, a tooth must be extracted, the process is very difficult and the horse usually needs to go to a horse hospital.)

The teeth a horse loses include his baby incisors and his baby molars. The baby incisors come out pretty easily, but often the baby molars hang around for awhile. Frequently a baby molar will sit on top of the incoming permanent molar, and then it is known as a "cap." Caps will fall off on their own; however, you or your veterinarian can remove a loose cap and make the horse's chewing more comfortable.

A foal will get his first teeth--the two middle nippers--at the age of about two weeks. He should have all six of his incisors about the age of eight months.

A mature horse has 40 teeth, while a mare has 36. The stallion or gelding has "tushes," or pointed teeth between the incisors and molars. Tushes are not always found in mares.

When a horse gets his teeth, their size, shape and markings can tell you his approximate age. The poem on the next page is by Oscar Gleason (1892) and will help determine the number of candles for the birthday cake:

74 HORSES SELDOM BURP!

TO TELL THE AGE OF A HORSE

To tell the age of any horse,
Inspect the lower jaw, of course
The sixth front tooth the tale will tell,
And every doubt and fear dispel.

Two middle "nippers" you behold
Before the colt is two weeks old.
Before eight weeks, two more will come;
Eight months, the "corners" cut the gum.

Two outside grooves will disappear
From middle two in just one year.
In two years from the second pair;
In three the corners, too, are bare.

At two, the middle "nipper" drop;
At three, the second pair can't stop.
When four years old, the third pair goes;
At five a full new set he shows.

The deep black spots will pass from view,
At six years, from the middle two.
The second pair at seven years;
At eight the spot each "corner" clears.

From middle "nipper," upper jaw,
At nine the black spots will withdraw.
The second pair at ten are white;
Eleven finds the "corners" light.

As time goes on, the horsemen know,
The oval teeth, three sided grow;
They longer get, project before,
Till twenty, which we know no more.

Sometimes horses and mares will develop small, pointed teeth in front of the molars of the upper jaw. These teeth are known as "wolf" teeth. They don't often appear in the lower jaw, but they can.

If a horse has all his teeth, plus wolf teeth, he could have as many as 44, while a mature mare could have as many as 40.

Most of the time it is a good idea to have wolf teeth removed, since they will frequently bother a horse while he is carrying a bit.

Horses don't often need an orthodontist. Usually they don't have crooked teeth. On occasion, however, they'll have teeth that don't meet properly. If the upper teeth stick out in front of the lower incisors, this is called, "parrot-mouthed."

When the lower teeth are in front of the uppers, then it is called an "undershot jaw."

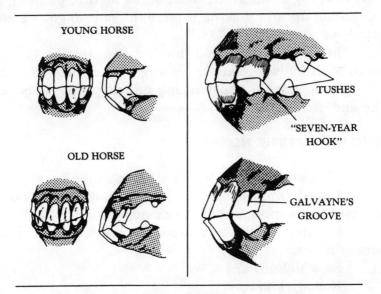

YOUNG HORSE

OLD HORSE

TUSHES

"SEVEN-YEAR HOOK"

GALVAYNE'S GROOVE

Both conditions are considered genetic defects, and horses with either condition should not be bred. Today, such conditions are not as serious as when virtually all horses grazed and had to bite off growing feed.

In the middle of all these teeth, a horse has a lot of tongue--12 inches or more--the major function of which is the intake of food.

A horse's tongue, like ours, does have taste buds, but unlike ours, it is not used in the production of sounds.

Horses do bite their tongues on occasion, but most often injury to the tongue is caused by heavy-handed riders and/or the use of severe bits.

Any serious cuts on the horse's tongue should be stitched, Dr. Alice says. Small cuts or insignificant scratches in the mouth generally heal well on their own.

You may have heard someone say a racing horse "swallowed his tongue" and couldn't get any air. That doesn't actually happen. What does happen is the horse balls his tongue up in the back of his mouth, pushing the soft palate up and making it more difficult to get a steady supply of air.

In addition to food intake and tasting, horses' tongues are also good for rolling the cricket in a bit, licking salt blocks, and sticking out at people they both like and dislike.

WHO KNOWS THE NOSE?

Who knows much about a horse's nose?

I don't think people who write books about horses pay much attention to the horse's nose.

I don't think veterinarians know much about horses' noses.

So who knows?

Nobody knows.

That may be a little hard-nosed, but it's true.

I know horses are pretty nosy.

I know the *Daily Racing Form* writes more about horses' noses than any other publication. Of course, the *Daily Racing Form* is wrong when it reports a horse won "by a nose."

Horses actually win races by "an upper lip." The horse's upper lips gets to the finish line before the nose, but it doesn't sound as good.

Upper lips are very special in their own right. They are extremely sensitive and can sort out and pick up the tiniest little piece of grain. They can curl and wiggle and flap and sometimes, but not often, they appreciate a little scratch.

Horse's noses are also a little deceitful. You don't see all that's there. There aren't just two nostrils; there are actually four.

When the "drinker of the wind" is taking in air, he does so through the same nostrils he flares. But he has other nostrils, inside the visible ones, which don't serve much of a purpose. In fact, I don't know the purpose, although I'm sure nature knows. (Dr. Alice doesn't know.) These interior nostrils are the false nostrils, and the only thing I know about them is that they vibrate. It's the vibrating of the false nostrils you hear when a horse is galloping hard, yet is relaxed.

Of course a horse uses his nose to smell. How important the sense of smell is to a horse is hard to tell.

We know a horse sniffs another horse when making his acquaintance. Or, at least we think one horse sniffs another. Mostly though, you'll find they blow more than sniff. And they blow into each other's nostrils.

An old horseman once told me if I'd blow gently into a strange horse's nostril, the horse would like me and not forget me.

I've been gently blowing into horses' nostrils ever since, but without any significant result.

As to the ability to detect odors, we are pretty sure the horse has a relatively keen sense. How much he relies on his ability to smell we are not sure, for he never just smells.

When a horse is investigating something, he uses his senses of sight and hearing in cooperation with his sense of smell. If you watch the horse closely, I suspect you'll never see him just look, or listen, or smell.

Of course, the most important function of the horse's nose is for breathing. A horse doesn't breath through his mouth. He always breathes through his nose.

Horses with great endurance or speed have nostrils capable of great expansion. Large nostrils facilitate large air intake.

When examining a horse, the observer should look carefully at the nostrils. At rest, the movement of the nasal openings should be even. There should be nothing spasmodic about their movement, says Dr. Alice.

When the horse is stressed, the nostrils should expand. The expansion should also be even rather than a sudden jerking open.

Horses are subject to nosebleeds. In most cases it is a condition known as "epistaxis," and is not considered too serious, according to Dr. Alice. The membranes of the nose are very delicate and richly supplied with blood. A sudden increase in blood flow can cause a rupture. This sometimes happens with race horses.

Race horses can also suffer a much more serious type of nosebleed, one caused by hemorrhage from the lungs. This is known as EIPH or exercise induced pulmonary hemorrhage, and must be treated to prevent infection in the damaged lung tissue, reports Dr. Alice.

Dusty, dry feed can cause a slight inflammation in the nostrils, which sometimes leads to a nosebleed. If this happens, there is usually very little loss of blood and almost immediate clotting.

The thing horses probably do best with their noses is stick them into other people's business.

No matter the breed, sex or age of a horse, you'll find he more often than not has his nose somewhere it doesn't belong.

His nosy tendency goes back to his natural curiosity, and to the fact that if he's going to look or listen, he's also got to smell.

For a horse, nose news is good news.

4
DOES HE LOOK HUNGRY?

Unfortunately, feeding the horse is not as simple as throwing a flake of hay over the fence.

When you get right down to the nitty gritty, no one really knows exactly what, or how much to feed a horse. Feeding a horse is both a science and an art. Neither is perfect; neither can do without the other. Still, it is always to the horse's benefit when the knowledge of science is guided by the art of horsemanship.

There are guesstimates as to how many megacalories of digestible energy the average horse needs under specific situations. It is pretty well understood how much digestible protein is needed by the average horse under certain circumstances, and it can fairly well be established how much calcium and phosphorus are needed daily. We think we know about how much salt intake is sufficient each day.

But when it comes to other vitamins and minerals, it's anybody's guess as to amounts required. Sure, there are some guidelines and published charts and tables listing the daily nutrient requirements of horses, but as complete as they may appear, they aren't the whole story.

Research on horse nutrition is increasing as the popularity of horse ownership increases, but horses aren't considered a major agricultural industry and so there is both limited interest and limited funding. New and accurate information is slow in coming.

If the average horseman attempts to feed according to any of today's acceptable daily requirement standards, he finds himself trapped in an impossible situation.

For example: how do you determine how many megacalories of digestible energy your horse gets each day? With the help of scientific instruments, you might be able to measure the horse's intake on a given day, but what about tomorrow?

The quality of the roughage (hay) fed changes from bale to bale, as does the quality of the grains (concentrates) being fed. Are you feeding sun-cured alfalfa, early-bloom, mid-bloom, full-bloom or mature? You can ask, but the feed dealer probably doesn't know the answer. Ninety-nine per cent of the time, you buy what is available and you feed it. On occasion, if the hay is moldy, or too wet or too stemy, you will send it back. In actuality, from day to day, the quality of hay varies bale to bale.

And the grain control problem may be worse. There is no question low quality grains are being marketed in various mixes. Heat used to dry grains destroys the seed life, and dead grain is less nutritious.

Only the largest horse operations, those with money enough to employ a full-time nutritionist, have any chance of preparing their own feed formula and regulating the intake of nutrients.

Even with the help of science, you can't be positive.

Blood tests and chemical analysis are helpful, but are far from the final answer in determining the efficiency of a horse feeding program.

So how do you determine the value of the grain you are feeding?

Actually, you don't. You rely on published charts to provide guidelines. You select the type of grains which are supposed to provide the amount and type of digestible energy a specific horse needs, and then you observe.

Most equine nutritionists and veterinarians tend to agree the best thing you can do is gain as much knowledge as possible about the feed you use and about the horse you feed. Then guess the nutritional requirements, giving careful consideration to the kind and amount of work the horse does.

Purchase only high quality feed to avoid contaminants, which not only endanger the horse's health, but can result in competition disqualification if prohibited substances appear in blood or urine tests. Store all feeds in safe, protected areas, and check frequently to be certain molds or other toxic elements are not present. Keep hay covered to protect it from sun and moisture.

So it comes down to understanding the science, then acting on the art. Look at the horse and make a judgment based on the way he appears, feels and acts.

Does the horse act healthy, interested and high-spirited? If he does, that's good. Is any feed left in the manger? If the horse is free-feeding, then there should be a tiny bit left. If absolutely every leaf or stem is gone, the horse may not be getting enough to eat. Then, of course, there are the overeaters. How much reserve fat is the horse carrying? The horse's ribs should appear covered. If the bones can be felt by rubbing your hand over the ribs with a light pressure, then the horse is in good condition. If you can't feel the bones, he is probably too heavy.

Performance horses are rarely, if ever, left on pasture, so we won't consider horses at pasture.

The stabled horse relies entirely on whomever is feeding him. Be sure the person doing the feeding understands exactly what and how much is needed.

By definition, hay is green forage with at least 85 per cent of its moisture dehydrated. The kind of hay (grass, cereal or legume) determines the protein value. The degree of curing (dehydration) affects the hay's weight.

A flake means nothing to a horse, and different things to different people. A child lifting a 10-pound flake of hay thinks it is heavy. A man may think it is too light. A flake of wet hay weighs much more than a well-cured flake.

If you can't determine the amount of hay being fed daily, then get a small scale and have the person doing the feeding weigh out the hay. Remember, the amount of water in the hay will determine its weight, and that can vary day to day, bale to bale.

Grass hays and some of the cereals are fed free-choice, meaning the horse has grass available all the time. Legumes (alfalfa and clover) are usually fed two or three times a day. A rough rule is one pound of early cut, high protein roughage for each 100 pounds of horse. A 1,000-pound horse gets 10 pounds of hay daily. That may not seem like enough, so if you are not sure of the quality of the hay, feed grass or cereal hay free choice as a morning feed and see how much the horse eats. If the horse is leaving the grass, then 10 pounds of the legume is plenty. (A horse will usually develop a hay belly as a result of being fed an over-mature legume sooner than it will from simply being over fed. Overfed horses will get fat all over.)

A mature horse on light work (up to three hours per day) will need 1.5 to 2 per cent of his body weight in feed per day. So a 1,000-pound horse will need 15 to 20 pounds of high protein hay (alfalfa or clover) per day. He will need more if he is on grass hay alone.

If a performance horse is getting 10 to 15 pounds of hay per day, then grains should make up the remainder of the horse's daily feed requirement.

Grains are fed to working horses and judged by the amount of work. Determine the grain to be fed by the amount of digestible energy desired. For example, corn can be fed in much smaller volume than oats because it has a much higher amount of digestible energy.

Some performance horses should be on low energy diets while others need to be on high energy rations. The energy level desirable for the horse must to be determined by the trainer.

A good place to start and from which to adjust the grain intake is with the 1,000-pound horse getting 10 pounds of legume hay plus some grass hay. If the horse is not being worked, or worked only lightly, this horse can start with about five pounds of oats per day.

For years, horsemen have fed grains by volume-- either quarts or gallons--which is nonsense. You measure the intake in weight based on the weight of the horse, not on the volume of the horse. In addition, volume measurements make no allowance for the differences in weight and energy provided by different grains. A quart of oats and a quart of corn are definitely not the same, and should never be fed as equals.

The feed value of oats depends on the kernel to hull ratio. The kernel is what is of value. The hulls are useless to the horse. Oats weighing 24 pounds to a bushel are more hull than kernel in comparison to oats weighing 40 pounds to the bushel.

Barley has a higher energy level than oats because of its reduced hull. It is 15 per cent higher in energy than oats.

Corn has an energy level 23 per cent higher than oats. Corn for horses should be rolled or fed on the cob, not cracked.

Wheat is the highest energy level grain and is not often fed to horses. It should be fed very carefully, if at all, because it is high in protein (most of which the horse should be getting from hay), low in calcium and moderate in phosphorus.

Milo is 13 per cent higher in energy than oats. Milo, if ground, should be mixed with molasses. It should also be mixed with bran or alfalfa as it is slightly constipating.

Wheat bran is an excellent laxative source, but should be fed sparingly. Rice bran can be used as wheat bran, but cannot be stored for long periods. Beet pulp is much the same as barley and adds bulk to the ration, as does corn cob meal. Molasses is usually added to hold grains together and add flavor. Levels should be kept below 10 per cent of the ration as molasses is laxative. Cull feeds, such as carrots, add moisture and sugar, but are laxative and should be limited and introduced slowly.

A mature performance horse needs a protein level of about 12 per cent daily, and should get it from a normal feeding of alfalfa or clover. Both are high in protein, but the level can vary depending on the cutting and amount of curing. Horses on a low-level protein diet should be fed two to three per cent of their body weight daily to insure sufficient protein.

Lactating mares, foals and young growing horses have a higher protein need. Try to get the mare and nursing foal a protein level of 20 per cent, while weanlings should be on about a 15 to 18 per cent level. Two-year old horses need a protein level of about 12 to 14 per cent. The protein need drops to 10 to 12 per cent about the time the horse reaches four years of age.

Horses getting more protein than actually needed will show it in their high energy attitude, or in high water consumption and frequent urination. Reducing the amount of alfalfa (replacing it with a grass hay) will usually reduce both the energy level and water consumption.

SUPPLEMENTS: NEEDED OR NOT?

A confirmed dietary deficiency should be the rule before supplemental feeds are introduced.

Many protein concentrates used as supplements are high in phosphorus and low in calcium. This can upset the natural balance of the two minerals. Calcium and phosphorus are required in ratio to each other: the ratio should never fall below 1.1 to 1, calcium to phosphorus. A good ratio is 1.5 to 1, calcium to phosphorus. Mature horses can tolerate 3 to 1 or even 5 to 1, but young horses cannot. Calcium deficiency can result in rickets and malformation of the head. Calcium overdoses result quickly in epiphysitis, a condition in young horses characterized by hard, localized swelling in the joints of the lower leg. Cutting down the young horse's alfalfa or clover (high in calcium) and increasing grains (high in phosphorus) will usually correct the situation.

Soybeans are generally considered a good supplement since they are high in lysine, an amino acid sometimes lacking in the regular diet, and low in calcium.

Linseed is very popular because it adds a nice gloss to the horse's coat. But linseed is more laxative than other supplements. Cottonseed meal or cakes can cause problems for young horses, but are used to add calcium. Safflower meal offers little of benefit. Sometimes it is hard to get horses to eat it.

Dried milk is an excellent source of calcium, but is very expensive in comparison to soybeans, for example. Some breeders add dried milk to the feed of young foals. Fish meal is good for protein, but is expensive and adds little else of benefit.

VITAMINS FROM A TO MINERALS

Vitamins do not provide energy, as too many horsemen believe. They do act as a catalyst, regulating the horse's ability to utilize other nutrients.

Vitamins come in two forms: water soluble and fat-soluble. Fat-soluble vitamins can concentrate in toxic proportions more easily than water-solubles because they are stored in the body while excess water-solubles are more easily removed by excretion in the urine.

Most of the time there is no need for vitamin supplements, according to Dr. Alice.

The precise functions of vitamin A are not known. A deficiency usually shows up as eye problems, skin problems, or lowered resistance to infection. Carotene, a substance found in all green, yellow and orange plants, is converted into vitamin A. A horse getting good cured hay will not need vitamin A supplements.

B-complex vitamins are popular, but need more study to determine exactly the role they play in horse nutrition.

In general, the B-complex vitamins are synthesized by the horse's digestive tract. The more work a horse performs, the more B-complex it will require. Green forage and good young hay provide B-complex vitamins.

Deficiencies in B1 and B2 appear as a loss of appetite, loss of weight, loss of condition or digestive tract problems. B12 is most publicized as helping with production of red blood cells and the prevention of anemia. But B12 injections are rapidly voided into the urine.

There is little to suggest the horse needs vitamin C supplements.

Horses not in sunlight for several hours a day should be given vitamin D supplements. However, they must be carefully regulated as overdoses result in irreversible calcification of soft tissue.

Vitamin E is probably a requirement of the horse, but is satisfied through the intake of green roughage.

Vitamin K helps blood to clot. Horses racing or running barrels or involved with distance competition suffer from "bleeding," a condition brought on by the stress of the exercise. Unable to handle the increased blood pressure during exercise, the horse's capillaries rupture and heart valves leak, allowing blood into the lungs, throat and sometimes into the nasal passages. "Bleeders", as they are known, can be aided by vitamin K and by the use of the diuretic Lasix, which reduces the horse's body fluids.

Minerals are divided into two groups: major minerals, used in quantity by the horse, and trace minerals measured in parts per million, says Dr. Alice.

Salt is the most common mineral provided to the horse. A horse should have a salt lick or granular salt available all the time.. A salt block put in the manger once a year plus the salt in prepared grain mixes, may not be sufficient.

The average horse needs 50 to 60 grams of salt per day. On a warm day, he can easily lose that much through sweating and urination. If he is worked, even moderately, he'll lose more. It will take about a four-ounce intake of salt to replace the loss. Observe the horse's condition and behavior. If the horse is chewing wood or licking the ground, salt may solve his problem.

Calcium and phosphorus have already been reviewed.

Magnesium supplement is normally not needed for a horse. In some areas, where cattle suffer from grass tetany, 5 per cent magnesium oxide can be added to salt to protect horses.

Of the trace minerals, sulfur is adequately supplied if the horse is getting enough protein. Iodine deficiencies are limited to certain geographic areas, usually those near large inland bodies of water. Iodized salt will solve the problem.

Selenium deficiencies, just as iodine, are limited to geographic areas. If you know that hay you are using was grown in such areas, selenium supplements are recommended.

Cobalt, a part of vitamin B12, need not be added to the diet.

Copper deficiencies are seen as anemia and knuckling over--joints popped forward due to contracted tendons. Enough copper is usually present, but other minerals are interfering with its utilization. A .5 per cent copper oxide salt will often solve the problems, but check with a veterinarian for dosages, Dr. Alice advises.

Iron is required by horses, and there are some iron-deficient growing areas for hay. Ferrous sulfate or ferrous chloride can be supplements.

Today, over-dosing of vitamin supplements is more of a problem than mineral deficiencies. Over supplementation can result in contracted tendons, epiphysitis, intestinal stones and muscle problems such as "tying-up."

In addition to getting minerals in feeds, horses get minerals in their water supply, and this must be taken into consideration.

One of the best ways to help your horse get the full value from his diet is to de-worm the horse on a regular basis. Ask a veterinarian for suggestions on a de-worming schedule and the drugs to be used.

The basic rules of feeding will contribute greatly to the horse's well being and ability to work.

1. Provide plenty of cool, clean water. Water should always be available, but if on occasion this is impossible, water before feeding.

2. Roughage (hay and grass) should make up the bulk of the horse's feed supply. Pellets are not good roughage. Hay cubes provide nearly the same roughage requirements as baled hays.

3. Feed small amounts often. It is best to feed three times a day. Twice a day is a minimum. Give the bulk of the horse's ration as the evening feed.

4. Adjust the feed to the work being performed.

5. Change feeds gradually. A new arrival of hay can drastically affect the horse's digestive tract and quickly

cause colic. Examine all new feeds and determine how to introduce the new feed.

6. Do not work a horse when his stomach is full. The stomach distends when full and presses on other organs, inviting colic. Work also causes the horse's energy to be diverted, slowing the digestive process.

7. Feed at regular times. Horses know exactly when it is dinner time, and they resent being made to wait. Regular feeding promotes regular digestion.

8. Add succulents daily if possible. Carrots, apples, even lettuce, provide the kind of juicy foods a horse loves. A pound of carrots per day is a good substitute for pasture.

9. Adjust feed to climate. Horses in hot climates will not need much of a reduction in the amounts of feed, but may well need additional salts. Horses in very cold climates burn hundreds more calories just staying warm, so they will need higher intakes of fiber (such as hay) than horses in warmer areas.

By the way, horses have lived on some very strange foods, from dried fish to sea weed. And they will drink a soda pop, which does tend to make them burp.

HORSES SELDOM BURP

Horses seldom burp!

A real rogue, who has no social conscience and most likely has been gulping air along with his food, will, on occasion, burp.

But for the most part, horses don't. It's not that they are so darned polite. It's that their digestive system is geared for one-way traffic only, and burping is therefore against their nature.

The equine digestive system plays a major role in the horse-mankind relationship. It was actually his digestive system which helped the horse become a working partner for man rather than man's dinner.

Cattle were the first work animals, and horses the supply of meat and milk. But the digestive system of cows made it necessary for them to lie down and ruminate (chew their cud) during working hours. All these short breaks slowed progress, so man switched his attention to horses which don't need "digestive time off."

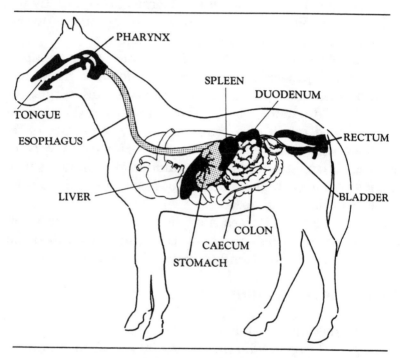

The horse's digestive system is made up of the alimentary canal--a muscular tube extending from the mouth to the anus--and the accessory organs, which are teeth, salivary glands, liver and pancreas.

The mouth is the initial section of the alimentary canal. The horse is a polite, slow eater, and will spend quite a bit of time chewing his food. During the chewing, the food absorbs saliva, which aids in swallowing and triggers a chemical reaction that starts digestion of starches and sugars.

Food passed from the mouth to the next section, the pharynx, is trapped. It cannot return because at the rear of the mouth is the soft palate, a kind of curtain separating the mouth from the pharynx. The soft palate opens only on swallowing and, in effect, provides a one-way flow of food. (This is also the reason a horse can't breathe through his mouth, as can so many other animals.)

The pharynx sends the food on to the esophagus, which is 50 to 60 inches long and runs down the left side of the horse's neck to the stomach.

The muscles of the esophagus work in successive waves of constriction, sending the food into the stomach. Because the constriction waves of the esophageal muscles can work in only one direction, it is nearly impossible for the horse to vomit. Anything that gets into the esophagus is going to the stomach.

The stomach is a muscular sac located in the abdominal cavity. The stomach is small in comparison to the size of the horse. This is attributable to the fact the horse is a constant eater with no need for large capacity.

The stomach works in a compressive manner and also provides some digestive enzymes. But food begins passing out of the stomach as soon as the stomach is approximately two-thirds full.

The small intestine is about 70 feet long, and it continues the digestive process, adding enzymes from the pancreas and bile from the liver.

The large intestine is last. It is divided into four parts: the caecum, large colon, small colon and rectum. The greater size of the large intestine allows the food to move along more slowly while final digestion takes place.

A system of veins along the large intestine channel the greater portion of food-enriched blood to the liver, which is the major chemical conversion plant. The liver regulates the distribution of the nourishment.

While not too complicated, the digestive system of the horse does require some special care. That care is primarily seen in the horseowner's feeding program.

The time of feeding, quality and amount of food, provision of adequate water and manner of feeding are vitally important to the good health of the horse and normal functioning of his digestion.

If the feeding program is bad, it's tough on the horse.

There's no "plop, plop, fizz, fizz" for the horse's upset digestive system. And he seldom gets the relief of a good burp!

PURE POISON

Bargain hay or hay cubes are no bargain if they kill your horse.

As the price of hay increases, a study by the University of California shows the number of horses being poisoned by contaminants in hay is also increasing.

And as the price of hay goes up, as a rule, down goes the quality and amount of hay being fed. A horse that is getting a low quality hay, or not enough, often starts looking for anything to munch.

There are no fewer than 18 deadly plants horses frequently find to munch.

In hay, the two most common are fiddleneck and groundsel. Fiddleneck is a problem only during the first cutting of a new stand of alfalfa. Groundsel can be a first-cutting contaminant in the second year, or even in older stands.

On the west coast, the common oleander plant accounts for a number of poisoned horses each year. One of the famous Budweiser Clydesdales died from oleander poisoning in a matter of hours. While being led past an oleander plant, the horse grabbed a mouthful of leaves. That was enough.

Castor beans are another common killer of horses. The castor bean is found most often in the southern regions of the U.S.

Other deadly plants are: Chokecherries, which are found most often in woods, prairies and orchards. They are large shrubs or trees and have pink and white flowers.

Bladder pod, or rattlebox, which has flat pods and yellow flowers. It is most common in the eastern and central states.

Death camas grows in low grazing land and are frequently found in hay. This is an herb with a grass-like leaf.

Staggergrass or staggerbush, is a spring and summer herb with a white, cone-shaped flower. Horses can get at it when they are being given a treat and allowed to graze in natural pastures.

Horse nettle is a summer and fall plant that looks a lot like a tomato plant.

Jimson weed is usually found in well-worn pastures, and Johnson grass is found all year long, especially in the south. Johnson grass is a coarse grass with a white vein.

Ivybush is an eastern and northwestern shrub with a rose-colored flower.

Laurel cherry is found in the southern regions. It has a heavy cherry odor.

Milkweed grows all year long, especially along roadsides. It has a long silky pod and produces a milky sap.

There are a number of sorghum grasses found throughout the U.S. Sudan grass is one common variety.

Yellow star thistle is found in the west, while yellow jasmine is found in the east. Both are deadly.

Water hemlock is a spring plant found in very wet open areas.

The best way to avoid these poisonous plants is by not letting your horse nibble while going on trail rides.

If you put your horse out to pasture, check with your State Department of Agriculture, which can provide helpful detailed information about poisonous plants. Then check the pasture carefully.

Don't buy bargain hay; buy from reputable dealers or feed stores. When you do buy hay, always open a bale or two and check it for contaminants. If you find a lot of foreign matter in the hay, reject it!

And upon the first signs your horse isn't feeling well--he may show colic signs, or stagger about, or get extremely nervous or tense, call a veterinarian.

There is seldom a cure, but immediate attention can sometimes save a horse from plant poisoning.

COOL, CLEAR WATER

When pure, it is odorless, tasteless, transparent.

Without it, life on earth is impossible.

It is one of the best solvents. It makes up the greater proportion of the horse's body, and he likes to keep it that way.

It's chemical formula is $H2O$. It's water, and more horses than not don't get enough, at least not enough of the right kind.

Without food, a horse could live about 50 days. Without water, he might live about 12 days.

Even the novice horseman gives careful consideration to the type and amount of food his horse gets, and there are plenty of vitamin and mineral supplements on the market to keep the average horseowner busy for years guessing what might be needed. (Most likely, none.)

But who stops to make a careful appraisal of his horse's water supply? There are more horses in poor condition through lack of sufficient water than through lack of sufficient food.

There are three things to consider in providing the horse with water. How much he gets, when he gets it and what kind he gets.

A 15 to 16-hand horse that is stabled, not doing hard work, and eating dry food, needs about 12 gallons of water each day during fairly cool weather. If the weather is hot and the horse is working hard, you can figure on doubling that amount.

A constant supply of fresh, clean water is best. The horse can then drink in the amount he wants whenever he's thirsty.

The horse's stomach has a lot to do with making this the preferred arrangement. The horse has a small stomach for his size, and the exit of the stomach is directly opposite the entrance and is larger than the entrance. So if you give water to a horse that has already started to eat, the fluid will wash undigested particles of food out of the stomach and into the intestines. This frequently results in colic, not to mention the fact that the digestive juices necessary for absorption of food will be diluted to such a degree that they may be rendered nearly ineffective.

Therefore, if the horse does not have free access to water, he should be watered before he is fed, never right after feeding.

It is also a poor idea to water a horse just before working him. The horse's stomach does not lie on the belly wall, but is suspended within the body of the horse. It lies against the diaphragm, which separates it from the lungs. If the stomach is filled with water or food, the capacity of the lungs to take in oxygen is reduced, and the horse will be under greater strain, which could lead to broken wind.

Contrary to popular belief, a horse may be given a drink while he is being worked, even if he is sweating. A horse that is hot from work can be allowed to drink, even cold water, providing the handler keeps the horse moving until he has cooled down. The mistake is not in letting the horse drink, but in giving him a drink and then not cooling him out properly.

Just like the rest of us, the horse needs clean, fresh water, not dirty, stagnant or tainted water.

The automatic water device has many advantages. It gives the horse all the water he wants when he wants it. It saves time for stable hands and it generally assures that the water is clean and fresh. However, automatic waterers must be checked to see they haven't accidentally been plugged and that the bowl is clean.

Automatic waterers must not be positioned so they get a lot of direct sun during the summer. Usually the water bowl is relatively small and the water will heat and discourage the horse from drinking. In addition, metal parts can become so hot they can burn the horse's muzzle.

Thirty-gallon plastic trash barrels also make good water containers for horses. If checked twice a day, they provide a constant supply of water, and if they are cleaned regularly, the water stays fairly fresh. In addition, horses have a difficult time breaking them or getting themselves hurt.

Using the old-fashioned common watering trough is a bad practice since it is usually not cleaned often enough and consequently provides an excellent means of spreading disease from one horse to another.

Every time you're thirsty, give a thought to your horse. He doesn't need a cola or an un-cola or a V-8. All he needs is a drink of fresh, clean water.

LOTS OF CHEW, NO NUTRITION

When horses aren't kept as busy as little beavers, that's exactly what they become. And their wood sculpturing isn't highly appreciated.

Besides being detrimental to the appearance of wood fences and stall doors, wood chewing is a costly vice that can be quite dangerous to the horse. Splinters in the horse's stomach and intestines can cause colic, infection and internal bleeding. Deaths linked to wood chewing are not unusual.

Wood chewing and cribbing are not the same. When a horse cribs, he places his teeth on a handy object--a fence or stall door, then he sucks in air, filling his stomach and ruining his appetite. Cribbers generally show poor condition, have enlarged muscles in the throat just behind the jaw and severely wear away their teeth.

Cribbing is such a bad vice, most horse sales make it mandatory the seller report the vice or the sale can be nullified.

There are cribbing straps (its like a belt which fits around the horse's throat to keep him from expanding it) and other devices designed to stop cribbing, but few are truly effective.

Wood chewing is generally a habit the horse develops out of nervousness or boredom. But it can also be a symptom of another serious problem. It can mean the horse lacks certain nutrients in his diet, or his feed does not satisfy his natural desire for roughage.

What contributes to making our lives easier is not always good for the horse, and we often fail to recognize the needs of the horse.

Examples of human thoughtlessness that can lead to wood chewing include feeding the horse pellets instead of roughage, using small box stalls and not giving the horse sufficient exercise.

From the owner's viewpoint, pellets are a convenient form of feed. But many studies indicate that horses fed pellets develop a strong urge to chew after their appetites have been satisfied. The only experiment I ever conducted with pellets proved to me that the more extensive research is correct.   It is not necessarily that the pellets lack nutrition--they simply don't satisfy the urge to chew.

Keeping horses in box stalls certainly makes their care a lot easier, and, for some owners, stalls or small pens may be the only solution to lack of space.   But the 12X12-foot structure doesn't make sense to the horse.

Being confined in a small place can have negative psychological effects on the horse.   He cannot see all the activity, normally quite interesting to the average horse.   He cannot run and play at will, and he cannot graze over great distances.   Wood chewing becomes a way in which the stalled horse demonstrates his displeasure with his cozy cottage.

Nervousness caused by lack of exercise often results in wood chewing.   The horse simply has excess energy that he can't get rid of.   Eventually, he finds the wood chewing relieves some of the tension, just as many humans get rid of their nervous frustration by biting their nails.

If wood chewing indicates the horse is missing a nutrient, it is usually salt, says Dr. Alice.   Be sure the horse has free access to a salt block, or is fed about a handful of table salt each day.

If lack of roughage is causing wood chewing, a return to hay may solve the problem, unless the vice has become a habit.   According to Dr. Alice, a horse's minimum hay requirement per day is one percent of his body weight, or 10 pounds of hay per 1,000 pounds of body weight.   Dr. Alice suggests, however, that with a wood chewer, feed enough hay at each feeding so the horse still has about a handful left by the next feeding.   If the horse is becoming to fat, Dr. Alice says replace some of the hay with grass.

Horses fed hay rather than pellets or hay cubes usually spend more time eating.   Consequently, they have less time for wood chewing.

Reducing nervous tension, eliminating boredom and supplying the proper roughage and nutrients are the only satisfactory solutions to the wood chewing problem.

Solutions that are dangerous, costly or ineffective after a short period of time include the use of Tabasco sauce or other hot spices, covering stall doors or fence rails with woven wire or metal strips, or electrified wire.

EVERYONE LIKES A TREAT

Every year we celebrate holidays with special meals. Why shouldn't our horses?

They should and can!

Treats for horses are good for horses, nutritionally and psychologically. (Note of caution: just like treats for humans, treats for horse shouldn't be overdone. Too much of a good thing can result in a tummy ache.)

We like to start our holiday meals with an appetizer. So do horses.

Before the main course of hay, let's tickle his palate with some sliced carrots, a big sticky gob of honey or molasses, some sugar cubes or even sliced fruit.

If not fed in overly large amounts, all are good for the horse, and will certainly stimulate his desire to eat. In fact, these appetizers are good for poor eaters anytime, says Dr. Alice.

If you think you get tired of Hamburger Helper, just think how tired a horse gets of hay. A little appetizer a half hour before mealtime can really perk him up.

Of course, Dr. Alice adds, you should try to discover why the horse is a poor eater and correct the problem. It may just be a monotonous diet, but it could be nerves, stress, poor health or a lack of exercise.

Now for that special meal:

Roots bring toots of happiness as a first course.

Carrots are the basic root. Add some parsnips, rutabagas, turnips, potatoes or sugar beets in small amounts and you've got a really delicious beginning. When preparing the roots, be sure they are cut finely enough to keep the horse from choking.

If you're not inclined to go with the roots as a first course, how about a special relish?

Pumpkins, squash and melons, sliced and in small amounts, are excellent. And don't worry about the seeds. When fed in small amounts, the seeds are not harmful to horses. Such fruits contain only six to 10 percent dry matter, so the nutritional value is low in comparison with cereal grains. Therefore, the horse still needs plenty of hay as a main course.

Entree: hay and grass. (Maybe a special hay for the day.)

If your horse doesn't normally get grain, then he'll surely enjoy a pound or so with his hay to make the meal sumptuous.

And if you want to add a tantalizing sauce, pour on some molasses or honey. If you just want to jazz up the normal meal a little, sprinkle the hay with sugar.

Dessert is always special to a horse, especially if it is a fruit compote.

Desserts, as always, are small. An apple a day is a good guiding rule. But on special occasions, throw in a plum, a pear, a peach or a nectarine. Be sure the pit has been removed from stone fruits prior to serving.

And when the special holiday meal is done, you want your after-dinner mint, and so does your horse.

According to my daughter, Cathy, Polos, (English candy mints) are the best, but they are hard to find in the U.S. She says peppermint Life Savers are almost as good.

One mint is enough for me.

Most of our horses, however, are not satisfied with fewer than three.

5
WHAT'S NORMAL?

When I was feeling a little sick, or ran a temperature or had a touch of the well-known "Pip," my mom would put me to bed and give me a little chicken soup.

Chicken soup, of course, cured everything!   It apparently still does.

But there's no such miracle cure for horses.

Rest, good food and fresh water, plus a tincture of time constitute the basic cure for horse ailments--for horses, it's the closest thing to chicken soup.   When the problem requires greater medical attention, call your veterinarian, says Dr. Alice.

How do you know when to call the hoss doctor?

By reading the horse's vital signs: temperature, respiration and pulse, Dr. Alice answers.

As you get to know your horse well, you'll recognize immediately when he isn't feeling up to par.   That's the time to check the signs.

The normal temperature for a horse is 99 to 100 degrees.   A temperature of 101 degrees is common in young foals, and the horse's temperature is normally slightly elevated in late afternoon.

A horse with a temperature is sick.   A horse with a temperature over 104 is usually very sick, Dr. Alice warns.

To check the horse's temperature, shake the thermometer to get the mercury down, then lubricate the thermometer and insert it full length into the horse's rectum.   (Before inserting, it is a good idea to attach a long string to the top of the thermometer. Hang on to the string and the thermometer won't be lost.

The thermometer should be left in for at least three minutes. (Once you take the thermometer out, read it. You do know how to read it, don't you? Practice rolling it until you can get an accurate reading every time.)

The respiration rate is the number of times a horse inhales and exhales each minute. (That's two actions for one rate.) The average rate for the complete cycle for a horse at rest is 16. But that is an average and may not be normal for your horse. You'll have to check your horse's respiration rate over a three or four-day period to discover his normal at rest rate. This will give you something to measure against if you think your horse isn't well.

The best way to determine the respiration rate is to place you hand on the side of the rib cage and count the number of breaths taken in one minute. The average watch with a second hand will do the timing nicely. Another way is to stand back from the horse and watch the in and out motion of the rib cage, or the opening and closing of the nostrils, while timing in the same manner.

If the horse has just been worked or is excited, the respiration rate can climb to 30 or 40 and still be normal. The rate you want to know is the at rest rate.

The pulse rate, at rest, is normally just a little more than double the respiration rate. So a horse with a 16 respiration rate would have about a 36 pulse. Like the respiration rate, the pulse will increase with stress or exercise.

The pulse is the throb or surge of force in the artery as the heart pumps blood through the body.

The easiest location to find the pulse is usually the artery that runs along the inner side of the horse's jaw. Other convenient locations are at the back of the fetlock joint and the inside of the elbow.

It's a good idea to practice taking your horse's vital signs. The practice will not only help you to read the signs more easily, it will establish what is normal for your horse.

Take the vital signs at different times of the day and over a three or four-day period. Be sure to write down the results each time, Dr. Alice says. You'll find the signs are slightly different under different circumstances, but always fall into a three or four-point range. If there is a 10 point variance from normal, Dr. Alice says your "alert" button should be flashing.

The next time your horse doesn't look just right, you can take his vitals. If he's in the normal range, maybe all he needs is a little of the "chicken soup doctoring."

But if his vitals aren't normal, he'll need some help from your local veterinarian, and your veterinarian will be delighted you've already started the diagnostic procedure.

WHAT CONDITION IS HIS CONDITION IN?

When you really want to know what condition your horse's condition is in, you've got to do a little more than eyeball it.

The horse's general state of health is a good indicator of the horse's general condition, but it doesn't tell the whole story.

Most experienced horsemen know when a horse is feeling good. They know when a horse is on the muscle. They know when the horse is ready to put forth his maximum effort.

The problem is the condition of the horse's condition may not be at its maximum. The horse's maximum effort for his current condition may not be his peak potential. He may lose the race by a nose. He may show fatigue after 48 miles of a 50-mile endurance test. He may come up sore and sour after a weekend ride in the hills.

You can look at a horse and see he's in good condition. but you've got to check inside to determine if he's at his peak of condition.

Many of the measurements related to condition involve the circulatory system, which is made up of the heart (pump) and the vessels for carrying blood throughout the body. An analysis of blood--the fluid that carries oxygen, nourishes all cells, removes waste and fights disease, can give a good indication of the horse's stamina, or performance capability.

Measurements of the red blood cells are most frequently considered when attempting to determine state of condition of the equine athlete. Red blood cells carry oxygen, and without an adequate supply of oxygen to meet the requirements of working muscles, the horse simply will not have the stamina or strength to win.

One of the most valuable analysis is hematocrit value, commonly known as packed cell volume (PCV). PCV is a percentage count of the red blood cells, Dr. Alice explains.

The average well-conditioned horse will have a PCV of about 35 percent. A top performance horse in top condition will probably be closer to 48 percent.

The red blood cell count should normally measure between nine and 12 million cells per cubic millimeter for light horses, and from seven to 10 million for draft horses. A blood count lower than the guide is termed anemia. Anemia has many causes, but the first consideration might be given to nutritional deficiencies, and/or parasites (worms), according to Dr. Alice.

Serious diseases, such as heart disease or emphysema, can cause the red blood cell count to be higher than average.

Measurements of hemoglobin are indicators of the oxygen-carrying capacity of the blood and are considered an index to performance potential. The hemoglobin concentration is measured in grams per 100 milliliters of blood. Most horses have a normal concentration of between 13 and 15 grams per 100 milliliters of blood. Some research indicates that hemoglobin concentration and total blood volume can be used to predict racing performance and physical readiness of the horse to work.

White blood cell count is not ordinarily used to predict a horse's performance potential, but it can do so by calling attention to an adverse condition, Dr. Alice advises.

The normal white blood cell count is between 8,000 and 11,000 cells per cubic millimeter. If the count is higher, it usually indicates some type of bacterial infection, and consequently a reduced performance.

Blood tests should be taken by a veterinarian and the analysis done by a reputable laboratory. For them to be beneficial, the horseman needs several tests to determine what is normal for a particular horse. Once normal is established, improvements or problems can be charted.

Whether hot-blooded, cold-blooded or blue-blooded, the best condition is knowing the condition of the condition.

WHAT'S IT ALL ABOUT?

Why all the arguments and controversy about horse health care and choice of treatments?

"Greed and ignorance," says Dr. Alice. (Of course I'm married to her, how else do you expect to get an interview with truthful, blunt answers?)

Are acupuncture, moxabustion, massage, Reiki, or homeopathy adjunctive or alternative treatments?

Depending on who you ask, they are everything from wonderful and marvelous to useless and black magic.

"Actually," says Dr. Alice, who is both a licensed veterinarian and a certified acupuncturist, "they are complementary. All deal with the healing process which involves many things we don't necessarily understand about the nature of life and the energy of the life force.

If viewed as complementary, instead of as opposed to allopathic medicine, I'm positive all medicine and all patients would eventually benefit."

Dr. Alice says complementary treatments should be used to intervene before health problems become so well developed that surgery or pharmacological treatment is necessary to maintain life.

Veterinarians who oppose the use of acupuncture, Reiki, and homeopathic treatment, generally don't understand them and haven't made an effort to educate themselves, says Dr. Alice. "Most of the time, I believe, their opposition is based on a fear of losing income."

Acupuncture is a method of healing involving the insertion of needles into the body to manipulate "chi" (life force energy). Dr. Alice explains the body has physical aspects (surgery) chemical aspects (drugs) and energy aspects (acupuncture) which may need treatment. Treatment, she says, can be by complementary methods.

"My experience has been that most of what is termed alternative medicine has a preventative function.

Allopathic medicine, on the other hand, is directed at an existing condition."

Reiki is a method of healing which channels spiritual energy through the hands of the performing person to the body of the horse being treated. It is, says Dr. Alice, similar to what we call "therapeutic touch."

Massage feels good and induces relaxation which relieves muscle spasms, relieves anxiety and acts similarly to therapeutic touch.

Moxabustion is an acupuncture method in which heat is applied to the acupuncture needles through the burning of an herb, Moxa.

Homeopathy involves treating illness with substances which create the same symptoms as the illness. The remedies are refined to the point where all that is left is the energy of the original substance used to make the remedy.

Homeopathy is sometimes called "vibrational therapy" because it restores to the body tissue healthy vibration patterns.

Does all the competition between various horse health treatment methods mean we have less healthy horses today?

"I really don't know," Dr. Alice responds. "Horsemen in the past took care of health problems by themselves because health practitioners were not as readily available.

I also think horsemen of the past were more attuned to noticing problems. Taken care of early, the problem did not become a major health threat.

That is not to say today's horseowner is not as concerned or alert. Today, due to urban and societal constraints, we keep horses in less than desirable conditions. Many horseowners simply are not with their horses except on weekends or holidays."

Dr. Alice says before thinking medicine, horseowners should seek to provide their horses with plenty of fresh air, exercise and a nutritious diet.

"Horseowners should not be afraid to ask about, study, and consider all forms of health care.

Objections to, or claims for any treatment, without convincing explanation or evidence of thorough understanding, should be avoided," Dr. Alice advises.

OUCH!

Every time you turn around your horse has another cut, scrape, bump, lump, slash or puncture.

And you can be sure the new problem occurred moments before the show class, the race, the event or the pleasure ride began.

Sometimes the disaster needs a little loving care. Sometimes it needs some professional medical treatment. It always needs a little attention.

The first rule of first-aid for horses is to treat all injuries as soon as they are discovered, says Dr. Alice. The initial treatment may be minor, such as rinsing off the injury with clear water. In any case, you must make your first treatment in such a manner as to be of benefit to further treatment and proper healing.

Don't take action without thought. Putting the wrong medication on a wound may cause severe complications.

But don't move too slowly. Some injuries need emergency first-aid and professional treatment within hours.

Using a time frame may be the best way to determine whether or not you have an injury which simply needs care, needs emergency first-aid or needs professional medical attention, Dr. Alice says.

If your horse has a bleeding wound, the question is one of survival. A horse can lose a lot of blood, but not for long. A slow dripping or running of blood which lasts less than 10 minutes is not too serious. A heavy flow of blood which lasts longer than 10 minutes is very serious, and is an emergency.

Wounds without a lot of bleeding may be considered emergencies if you think they may need suturing. To delay getting a wound stitched may result in contamination, causing further complications. Leg wounds often fit into this category, according to Dr. Alice.

Wounds on the face and body may also need suturing. Have your veterinarian take a look as soon as possible.

All other wounds, scrapes, lumps and bumps are probably not emergency injuries, and fall into the "need professional attention" or "loving care" categories.

Major blows to the horse's body, which may not show much on the surface, can often be "need professional attention" candidates. A horse which falls, or runs into a fence or kicks a solid object, then shows some signs of lameness, or an inability to move normally, should be seen as soon as possible by your veterinarian.

Horses which scrape the hide off in a spot or two, or have a shallow cut which is not too long, generally need only loving care.

If the injury falls into the "needs first-aid" category, you must take two actions--call the veterinarian and apply the initial treatment while waiting for assistance.

In applying the initial treatment, you must do a combination of three or four things.

First, free the injured area of contamination as best you can. This usually means running cold, clear water from the hose on the wound. If running water is unavailable, get a bucket or pan of water and sponge the wound. If you can't do that, don't mess with it.

Second, continue to run cool, clear water on the wound to keep it clean and keep the swelling down. If you can't do that, don't mess with it.

If the wound is bleeding, you may apply a compress. A compress should be bulky, and can be made of clean towels. Emphasis is on pressure and clean.

Finally, determine the status of the horse's tetanus immunization. Your veterinarian will want to know. It is a very wise horseman who keeps the rules of first aid treatment in mind.

There is a final (in case all else slips your mind) rule I use.

If I faint, everyone calls everyone!

OH, MY TUMMY ACHES!

Colic is a killer, yet it isn't a disease.

It's a stomach ache--horse size!

Gas colics are most common, and they are easily treated by any horseman.   It's a matter of having the remedy on hand, or getting it quickly.

Colic is the name given to any undiagnosed abdominal pain the horse suffers.   In many cases, the horse is treated for colic and the specific cause of the trouble is never identified.

But we could significantly reduce the number of stomach aches if we dewormed our horses regularly, Dr. Alice believes. Bloodworms and the damage they do greatly increase the opportunity for colics.

Probably the most common colic is caused by a sudden change in feed.   Often the colic is mild, then over with and unnoticed by the horse's owner.

Horses should be introduced to new feeds gradually, especially lush, green feeds. Moldy feed can cause colic, as can an irregular and sporadic feeding schedule. Establish both the amount you feed and the time you feed and stick to the schedule.

Just as with people, colic can be caused by overeating, or the overeating can cause gas, which results in colic.

For gas colic, give almost any of the over-the-counter gas relief remedies humans use.   They are inexpensive and they work--rapidly. Infant's gas relief drops work great, and so do any of the adult liquid gas relief formulas if they contain simethicone.   Don't hesitate to give simethicone at the first signs of colic. If it is not a gas colic, no harm will have been done., says Dr. Alice.

Infant gas reliever has a dropper for administration. Give four or five droppersful, Dr. Alice advises.   Give 20 to 40 ccs or one to two ounces of the adult liquid gas relief. Be sure the horse swallows the medication.

Colic doesn't go away easily for the horse, for unlike a lot of human overeaters, the horse has a difficult time burping, and he can't vomit.

Other contributors to colic are cribbing, too much water after a hard workout, and poor teeth, which keep the horse from chewing his food properly.

A common cause of colic is sand impaction, which means the horse has ingested sand with his food. Do not put your horse's feed on the ground, and be sure the horse is getting enough to eat so he isn't sifting through the soil looking for a stem of hay.

No matter the cause, the signs of colic include restlessness and sweating. A colicky horse will often pace or paw, and frequently he will break out in a sweat.

If you ask your horse what's bothering him, he'll look at his sides, or he'll bite at his side or rub his sides against the wall or fence. If he is in severe pain, he may kick at his sides.

Certainly the horse with colic will not eat and most likely will not drink. He may moan a great deal, and if you put your ear to his side, you will not hear a lot of normal stomach noise. Under normal conditions, you'll hear the workings of the stomach and intestines, but when a horse is suffering from colic, normal digestion shuts down.

Finally, the colicky horse will frequently throw himself about in agony. He may try to get down and roll, which many believe can result in a twisted intestine. It is best to keep the horse up and moving.

At the first signs of colic, try the gas relief approach and keep the horse moving.

If there is no improvement in 30 to 45 minutes, call your veterinarian. Make the call, even though many cases of colic will disappear on their own. It's always better to be safe than sorry. You can always call back and cancel.

While you are waiting for the vet, walk or jog the horse. This may help to relieve a gas pocket. Don't overexert the horse. The idea is to relax him, not make him tired.

Ulcers can also cause colic. Ulcers are usually seen in young horses--yearlings, two and three-year-olds--under the stress of early saddle training or intense performance conditioning.

Horses with ulcer colic will show all the symptoms of gas or impaction colic, but will not usually show severe signs of shock, says Dr. Alice. If the anti-gas medication doesn't help, and the horse doesn't appear in too much distress, try Tagamet or other ulcer medications.

If you don't get a satisfactory result within a few hours, you need a veterinarian, Dr. Alice cautions.

When a horse has a tummy ache, act quickly, and get professional help, because colic can kill.

AN INTERESTING CONTRADICTION

There are all kinds of conceptual contradictions in the horse world, and inflammation is one of them.

Inflammation can be both good and bad at the same time.

And to relieve the bad effects of inflammation, horsemen often deliberately create more in the hope that what exists will be healed in a shorter length of time.

Inflammation is a reaction of the body to injury, and is commonly characterized by heat, redness, swelling, pain and disturbed function.

Since inflammation is a natural response of animal tissue to injury, inflammation is present every time the horse sprains, strains, bumps, twists, cuts or punctures some part of his body. It also occurs when the horse is attacked internally by viruses, bacteria, chemicals or parasites, says Dr. Alice.

The immediate reaction to an injury is usually swelling of the surface of the injured area of the horse's body; redness is also noted. The body sends an increased supply of blood to the injured area, much as we would send extra fire fighting units to a major blaze. Because the white blood cells are responsible for removing contamination and debris caused by the injury, a larger than normal supply is needed at the scene.

The purpose, then, of natural inflammation is to kill infectious agents, prevent the spread of disease, clean up the damage caused by the injury and heal the injured area.

But sometimes horsemen want to hasten the natural healing process.

This is done in two ways.

The first is to clean the injury and make it as free of contamination as possible. This creates the most advantageous climate for the body to heal itself.

Or, as some practice, a horseman may create additional inflammation intentionally by using an agent that actually causes more damage to the affected area, thus dilating even more blood vessels to assure an even greater supply of blood.

An example is blistering a horse if the animal has shin bucked. When a horse shin bucks, the tissue along the front of the cannon bone is damaged and natural inflammation is immediate. The application of a blister (through the use of a caustic agent) encourages additional swelling due to the increased blood supply, and it creates additional discomfort for the horse. The only good part about induced inflammation is that the injury often heals more quickly. (This is, of course, a matter of opinion. Personally, I don't believe it, since there is no way to prove the claimed benefits. I believe blistering or firing is ineffective, unnecessary and without any reasonable justification. But that is only my opinion.)

The horseman could also treat bucked shins with light exercise followed by a day or two of rest, thus preventing additional damage to the tissue. He could also cool the damaged area. This is accomplished by running cold water onto the cannon bones, reducing the swelling by deterring the increase of blood, thus lessening the pain associated with the inflammation. The use of cooling poultices can also aid in the healing process.

Given enough time, the natural healing process usually repairs or replaces the damaged tissues and restores good health to the area.

Ordinarily, when horsemen talk of inflammation, they don't use the term itself. They indicate what is inflamed by adding "itis" to the word for the affected area of the horse. For example, an inflamed tendon is called tendonitis, whereas an inflammation on the horse's skin would be dermatitis.

When a horse is injured, inflammation is beneficial because it is part of the natural healing process. At the same time, inflammation is bad because it creates swelling, congestion, pain and heat.

And inflammation is even more contradictory because horsemen often make it worse in an attempt to make it better.

NEW NAME, OLD PROBLEM

What used to be known as Monday Morning Disease and was incorrectly called azoturia, should be Performance Horse Syndrome, or more correctly "too much dietary calcium."

But today everyone calls it "tying up."

The name azoturia originates from azote, the French word for nitrogen, indicating an abnormal amount of nitrogen in the urine. That is usually not the case in horses tying-up, hence azoturia is an incorrect name for the condition.

The name Monday Morning Disease was applied years ago because so many work horses suffered the affliction when they went back to work following a weekend of rest.

Today the syndrome strikes on any day of the week, and it is seen most frequently in mares normally getting a consistent amount of healthy exercise and plenty of feed--in other words, "performance horses."

Dr. Alice explains that tying-up can occur in many different types of performance horses and for several different reasons. Tying-up, she adds, can happen when an endurance horse becomes exhausted or sweats excessively, resulting in an electrolyte imbalance.

Dr. Alice says many cases of tying-up, however, result from a metabolic disorder related to having too much calcium in the diet. The over-abundance of calcium comes from calcium rich alfalfa or calcium high supplements.

This overdosing of calcium leads to suppression of the parathyroid gland which regulates the calcium level in the blood, Dr. Alice explains. The suppressed parathyroid is unable to replace the large amounts of calcium used by nervous energy and muscle usage, and the muscles suffer tetany, sustained muscle contraction.

"As simple as it may sound, it is my experience that controlling the amount of calcium in diet eliminates tying-up," says Dr. Alice. Discontinuing supplements with calcium and feeding reduced amounts of alfalfa are usually all that is required, she adds.

Tying-up syndrome is characterized by muscle stiffness, especially of the hindquarters and loin, at times profuse sweating, reddish brown to almost black urine and obvious signs of pain.

Tying-up hits suddenly. The horse appears perfectly normal, maybe even a little on the "high" side when taken

118 HORSES SELDOM BURP!

from the stall. Shortly after exercise begins, the visual signs appear. The horse's breathing may be hurried, and muscle stiffness is evident. In severe cases, complete lameness in the hindquarters will probably occur, and the horse could go down.

The horse will not want to move. Don't move the horse, Dr. Alice emphasizes. Start helping the horse by leaving him right where he is. Then devise an effective plan to relieve pain and make the horse more comfortable. If possible, blanket the horse while waiting for veterinary assistance.

If the horse is not in too much distress, walk him slowly to his stall or corral.

Most veterinarians treat tying-up syndrome cases by first giving the horse a tranquilizer, which helps relax the muscles, plus an injection of vitamin E, calcium and selenium. The horse is then rested for a day, after which it can begin a very light exercise program.

The horse's diet may be changed, but usually in the wrong way. The calcium intake is not corrected. Instead many vets still recommend the horse not be given grain for a day or two, and then be given grain in small amounts, increased gradually each day.

Forget the old ways. If you want to avoid the tying-up syndrome, control the amount of calcium in your horse's diet. Try it, you'll like it!

BANDAGES SHOULD PROTECT

The other day a woman called me over and asked, "Would you check this bandage and see if it is right?"

"Why are you bandaging the horse?" I asked.

"She's kind of sore, and I want to work her."

I didn't ask why she wanted to work a sore mare. I looked at the bandage. It was a shipping boot applied over cotton.

"This is not an exercise bandage," I said. I took off the bandage from the left leg, and my gosh, what a surprise, the mare had a small bow. I took the bandage from the right leg. Same condition. I suggested she call her veterinarian before working the mare. "There could be a problem here," I said.

I suspect the woman found someone else to help her bandage the mare, and I suspect the mare, even though sore, was worked.

I've found that bandages such as bell boots and splint boots are often used for no specific reason other than they look good.

A professional bandage shouldn't have a look unless it's one of neatness. A professional bandage is not there to be seen. It's there to prevent bumps, nicks and scrapes, to protect an injury, or help a healing process.

It is not necessary that a bandage always be started in a certain place, or that it end in a certain place. What is necessary is that the bandage stays on and does the job it was intended to do.

The biggest danger with bandages is that they are misapplied--they are either so tight they cut off circulation or are not flexible enough to give with the movement of the horse.

Bandages put on by the novice horseman are often quite neat, and just as often serve no function.

The shipping bandage is the most common. The handler usually wraps the bandage neatly, (and of course it matches the color of the horse's blanket, the trailer and the gate post to the side paddock) but fails to cover the area most frequently injured--the pastern and coronet. Shipping boots are fine if they are pulled down over the pastern and coronet.

The best materials for wrapping the leg are heavy cotton sheets and heavy flannel strips. The strips should be about six inches wide. A good knit bandage can also be used.

It isn't necessary to wrap in a certain way, but the preferred method is to always wrap from the inside out. Start by placing the cotton on the inside of the leg in the groove between the tendon and cannon bone. Then bring the cotton forward, across the cannon, then around the leg. Do the same with the flannel strips. When pulling the bandage snug, pull across the cannon bone, not across the tendons.

Many old-time horsemen finished bandages with safety pins. While this has been done for years at race tracks, I'm thoroughly modern and like Velcro. Some horsemen still use tie strings, but there is a danger since they don't give with movement.

If braces or sweats are being applied to the horse, the same bandaging materials are normally used. (It is often common to cover the sweat with a plastic wrap, then cover with cotton.)

When medications are being applied, it is the wise horseman who checks carefully on the proper use of the paint or ointment, the need for additional protection and the length of time the bandage should be left in place.

I like to remove a bandage both morning and night just to make sure circulation is good and that the leg remains clean and is progressing as expected.

An exercise bandage should have some elastic properties so it can be pulled tightly enough not to slip. If cotton is used under the exercise wrap, then it must be thin sheet cotton. If the padding under an exercise wrap is too heavy, it can lump and cause excessive pressure in specific areas. Bowed tendons can be caused by bandages, hence the name, "bandage bow."

There are special bandages for special problems, such as the spider bandage for use on knees. Such bandages have very specialized uses, so be sure you know how and why before applying.

Before applying a bandage, ask yourself if it will protect the leg, guard against cuts, scrapes or bumps, or help the healing process. If it hasn't got a specific purpose, it doesn't look good. It looks out of place.

THE SAME, BUT DIFFERENT

There is very little difference between strangles and dry land distemper. Yet there are a lot of differences!

Strangles, which is distemper, is a bacterial respiratory infection caused by *Streptococcus equi.* Dry land distemper is an infection caused by *Corynebacterim pseudotuberculosis,* reports Dr. Alice.

Strangles is common throughout the U.S., while dry land distemper seems to be confined to the western states.

Strangles causes pronounced swelling (which can become abcesses) in the lymph nodes and glands in the area of the throat, which often cuts off the horse's air supply--hence the name, "strangles." Dry land distemper can also affect the lymph nodes of the throat, but frequently attacks the lymph nodes in the chest and groin. The sheath in males and mammory glands in mares may be involved, says Dr. Alice.

Today, strangles, with adequate treatment, is not usually a major threat to life. Dry land distemper is considered a rather mild disease, although uncomfortable for the horse. Both infections rarely lead to fatal internal absesses.

The horse with strangles will generally show signs of a stiff neck, a high fever, nasal discharge, a cough and a lack of appetite. The horse with dry land distemper will exhibit painful, hot swellings and occasional lameness, but usually doesn't run a high fever.

Strangles is a highly-contagious disease and is spread by purulent material from ruptured lymph nodes and nasal discharges. It can be ingested by a healthy horse or inhaled as droplets. Common water troughs, feed buckets, blankets and brushes can be sources of infection.

Dry land distemper is infectious, but not highly contagious. It is spread by flies that bite both diseased and healthy horses along the ventral midline (belly).

The similarities and the differences are easily recognizable, but positive proof that a horse has one or the other of the diseases can only be determined in a laboratory. Material from an abscess must be analyzed.

It is important a veterinarian be consulted when a horse shows signs of either disease, since proper action early will usually prevent any serious complications or permanent after effects.

The great problem with either disease is the possibility of internal infections, which can be serious.

If strangles or dry land distemper is suspected, the horseowner should request an examination by a veterinarian. While waiting for the vet's visit, the horse should be treated as if the problem were strangles.

Isolate the horse immediately. And don't give antibiotics without first consulting your vet. In many cases, antibiotics will only slow down the natural process.

Your veterinarian may not prescribe medications, but may advise hot packs and/or external poultices to speed up the abscess process.

There are no preventive actions against dry land distemper except insect control, but there is a vaccine against strangles. However, Dr. Alice reports, the vaccine can have some ill effects and should be given only on the advice of your vet.

If you have horses, sooner or later you will see one or both diseases. Strangles is most common in very young horses, but, like dry land distemper, can attack a horse of any age.

Now that you know the differences, you know your first action should be to treat them the same.

THE MEDICINE CHEST

If you're like me, your medicine cabinet is full of a lot of things that can't be used, and only a few things which can.

It's the same with your horse's medicine chest. It's probably loaded with things no longer worth having. And what you need is probably buried or hidden by things which have dried out, been used up, or are too old to be effective.

The trick is to clean it out periodically. Then restock.

And don't overdo it! You really don't need as much as your horseochondriac thinks.

You'll need a thermometer. Get a good one. Thermometers are all hard to read. You can roll them in your fingers a hundred times and still not see the mercury. So select a thermometer on the basis of how easy it is to read. (A little practice will help, but where is the fun in that--it only makes you overly prepared.)

You'll need some blunt surgical scissors. It's not so much that you might need to protect your horse when you have to cut a difficult bandage from him; the blunt points are so you won't stick yourself when he moves.

You'll need several rolls of cotton. These are for leg injuries. Don't let them out of their wraps for any other purpose. Once a roll of cotton sees daylight, it will immediately jump into the dirt, tear itself and absorb hay, straw and shavings into its layers.

Rolls of cotton should be forbidden to move.

A small bag of cotton balls. (A small bag will last a thousand years since you won't use them often. They are primarily there to keep you from touching the rolls of cotton.)

Several rolls of gauze, at least eight quilted pads to use for leg bandages, four cotton knit leg wraps for standing bandages, some self-sticking tape wraps, some masking tape for holding wraps which won't stay in place, and some duct tape for use on feet.

A bottle of rubbing alcohol is required, as is your favorite non-irritating antiseptic topical dressing. You should also have a bottle of your favorite liniment. Horse liniments are used on sore and swollen muscles or on the legs to create circulation and give relief to stretched or pulled tendons and ligaments. I like a liniment that has a pleasant aroma, since I also like to have it rubbed into my sore back muscles.

It is a good idea to have a supply of clean rags, towels and soap. Dish soap in a plastic squeeze bottle is pretty good. The soap and towels can be used to wash your hands prior to and after treating a wound, and the rags can be used to scrub up a scratch or abrasion.

A little Vaseline or mineral oil is good as a lubricating agent. Either will work as a hoof dressing.

You'll need a cheap bottle of bleach for treatment of thrush and general cleaning of the bottom of the horse's hoof.

Some type of ointment as a topical dressing is nice to have. Old timers saved bacon grease and it still works better than most things, although it doesn't make most veterinarians happy.

I like to have a supply of Butazolidin tablets or paste. I keep them and my bottle of aspirin handy. This way both the horse and I can get some quick minor pain relief.

You should have a drawing salve such as Icthammol and some type of medicated poultice for cooling inflamed tissue or drawing hoof abscesses.

It is also an excellent idea to have Epsom salts for use in soaking feet when you suspect a hoof abscess.

A bottle of 7% iodine is a must.

I have a rule: Never give shots unless specifically directed by your veterinarian. I think it is a bad policy for the horseowner to administer medications. If a treatment requires follow-up--say the veterinarian wants you to give 20ccs of whatever each day for the next four days--well, then you do it. Otherwise, don't give shots. Don't keep needles or syringes.

Do keep a notebook and pencil handy. They are good for jotting down remedies, telephone numbers, shopping lists and the dates various medications were given your horse.

Invariably the veterinarian asks, "When was the last time Diablo had.....?"

You'll put Dr. Alice in shock if you check the notebook and reply, "You administered it on June 1 about 9:30 a.m. You were late again that day."

6
NOT UP MY NOSE WITH A RUBBER HOSE

While the chances of ridding your horse of worms are somewhere between slim and none, the chances of your horse dying from worm-related problems range from good to very good.

Some studies have indicated up to "fifty percent of all horses die directly or indirectly from internal parasites."

As frightening as that may be, there are some things you can do to reduce worm-related health problems and help your horse live a long, happy life.

You really don't need to know what to look for to determine whether or not your horse has worms--I can assure you he does. However, the most noticeable external signs are rough hair, a pot belly, fever, coughs, listlessness, diarrhea, dull or watery eyes and poor growth. Any of these signs, alone or in combination, indicate the worm problem could be severe.

But even if your horse has a shiny coat, is fat and appears to be quite healthy, he probably does have a worm problem.

Where your horse lives has a lot to do with his worm infestation. Horses in stalls or corrals are more apt to be infested than horses wandering over acres of pasture. And horses living in warm, moist climates are more at risk than horses living in hot, dry locations.

Cold weather isn't as big a help in reducing worm populations as hot weather. Cold, according to most research, does not break the parasite's life cycle because unlike heat, cold doesn't destroy worm eggs. When the temperature nears the 90 degree level, many parasite eggs are destroyed.

While there are more than 100 types of internal parasites, Dr. Alice says you need to concern yourself with *Strongylus vulgaris* (small and large bloodworms), *Ascarids* (roundworms), *Bots* and *Pinworms.*

Strongylus vulgaris gets its name, bloodworm, because as an adult, it sucks blood after it attaches itself firmly to the walls of the large intestine. It is while the bloodworm is attached to the walls of the intestine that the female deposits large numbers of eggs, which pass with horse droppings to the ground.

Once on the ground, the warm larvae hatch, then fasten themselves to grass or hay stems, which are eaten by the horse. Back inside the horse, the larvae migrate for about six months before returning and maturing in the intestines to reestablish the cycle.

In recent years, Dr. Alice says, small strongyles have replaced the large strongyles as the major horse parasite in many areas.

Small bloodworms burrow into the intestinal lining, causing ulcers, chronic inflammation and interfering with the horse's digestion, which often leads to chronic diarrhea.

The large bloodworm attaches itself to the intestine wall, sucks blood, can block blood flow and damages artery walls.

Bots, a fly larvae, damages a horse's tongue, lips and throat, as well as interferes with digestion once the larvae have attached themselves to the stomach wall.

Ascarid (roundworm) larvae will migrate through the horse's body, penetrating the intestinal wall, the liver and the lungs. Especially dangerous to young horses, roundworms can grow to be a foot in length and can block the intestine or puncture it.

Owners should give special attention to new foals, as roundworms will severely retard the absorption of needed nutrients, stunting the foal's growth. They may even block the foal's intestines, resulting in death. This can, and has, happened to foals as young as three months. These worms can also cause pneumonia in foals since they migrate through the lungs.

Pinworms in large numbers can upset digestion and sometimes cause anemia. Pinworms are quite often the cause of "tail itch."

Worms are a problem all year long and are virtually impossible to eliminate because of the structure of their life cycle.

Deworming kills most of the adult and immature worms. However, there are still thousands of eggs remaining in the horse and ready to hatch at different times. In addition to the eggs, the migrating larvae, which move through the horse's body for six months or longer, most likely will not be affected by the medication. The larvae become adult worms, laying more eggs, while the other eggs are being passed out of the horse, then reswallowed to become new larvae.

Deworming programs should be aimed at interrupting the parasite's life cycle by inhibiting contamination of the environment as much as ridding the horse of the worms he already has, says Dr. Alice.

If everything you have read so far is scary, give some thought to this fact: The majority of horseowners don't know as much about worms as you have just read.

But don't panic. You can do a lot to minimize the parasite problem.

Because the life cycle of the worm is continuous, any worming program must also be continuous. Get the advice of your veterinarian and begin a regular health program immediately, Dr. Alice advises.

She also says it is not necessary today, and not even a good idea, to tube worm a horse. "Today's medications are extremely effective and can be given orally as a paste or as a feed additive. It is necessary for the horse to swallow the correct dose for his weight. One tube of paste wormer per horse doesn't work. There are occasions when passing a stomach tube through the nostril is required, but not for de-worming."

Thousands of horses are cheering because of Dr. Alice's advice, and proclaiming, "Not up my nose with a rubber hose."

It is Dr. Alice's recommendation you deworm your horse's every eight weeks. She suggests, however, you develop a parasite control program with the advice of your veterinarian.

TETANUS AND OTHER 'SHOTS'

I got bit by a horse.

He was a nice horse until he bit me. Then he was a mean, nasty, bad stallion, and I told him so.

The bite broke the skin; the wound bled, and then turned a nice deep purple.

Did I need a tetanus shot?

Every horseman should know the answer, but few do. I didn't, so I decided to ask members of my equine studies class of 30 men and women.

"You need a tetanus shot every year," one said.

"No, you don't," said another. "You'll be all right. Don't worry about it."

A young woman said, "If it broke the skin, you'll have to take the painful Pasteur treatment." She was obviously referring to the infamous Pasteur remedy for rabies, a malady I might have feared had I been bitten by a dog. (Horses also can, and sometimes do, contract rabies.)

NOT UP MY NOSE! 131

It was clear what had to be done. Ask Dr. Alice, then call my doctor.

Both Dr. Alice and my doctor agreed. Immunization against tetanus is very important, especially for horses and horsemen. Tetanus bacteria hate oxygen, like dirt and are thrilled by horse manure.

Tetanus is always around horses, says Dr. Alice, and it is a killer, so immunize your horses.

"Although tetanus is present with all wounds, it is much more common if the wound was made by a puncture," Dr. Alice says. "Tetanus bacteria like to get away from oxygen and do very well in a deep, contaminated puncture."

To protect your horse, you should start a toxoid program. This involves two injections of tetanus toxoid four to six weeks apart, and then booster shots at one-year intervals. It is wise to keep a record showing your horse's toxoid program is up to date.

There is a lot of confusion among horsemen about tetanus toxoid and tetanus antitoxin, according to Dr. Alice. One is safe, the other much less so.

Tetanus toxoid is quite safe, effective and long-lasting. The only adverse effect ever observed is an occasional and temporary swelling at the point of injection. On the other hand, tetanus antitoxin often gives excellent protection for two to three weeks, but its use sometimes results in serious and possible fatal after-effects, Dr. Alice warns. The problem with antitoxin is that it contains horse serum, and horse serum injections are too frequently followed by equine serum hepatitis, which can be fatal.

Why might a veterinarian be forced to use tetanus antitoxin in spite of its drawbacks? In the absence of records or knowledge that the horse is being protected by a current toxoid program, he must use the antitoxin because it gives immediate protection, whereas toxoid does not, unless the horse is on such a protective program.

Because of the risks of using antitoxin, it is wise to start your horse on a toxoid program and keep him on it.

The main symptom of tetanus is muscle stiffening. The animal has a rigid posture with the head and tail extended. Usually the first muscles affected are those of the jaws, thus the name, lockjaw.

In humans, the incubation period of tetanus is two to 50 days, according to my doctor. The most frequent symptom is, of course, a stiffness of muscles, especially in the jaws.

My doctor assured me I wouldn't get tetanus from the bite, while pointing out that the tetanus spore might be on my skin and thereby get into the wound. "Tetanus is dangerous and there are still a number of deaths from tetanus," he said, "chiefly among the young and old."

Most people should be immunized about every 10 years, but a person working with horses should be immunized every five years. If you suffer a wound, it should be washed immediately and then treated, he said.

The tetanus shot doesn't hurt when you first get the needle. It hurts the next day.

I got my shot in my arm. It's hard to sit on a horse when you've had a tetanus shot in your bottom.

In addition to tetanus, your horse should be protected against equine influenza, a very contagious disease caused by two of the viruses in the influenza A group. Influenza attacks the respiratory tract and is associated with cold symptoms.

Rhinopneumonitis is a mild disease of the upper respiratory tract. A particular strain of Rhino can cause abortion.

Encephalomyelitis is also caused by a virus, and we principally vaccinate against two: eastern and western. There is a third encephalomyelitis virus: Venezuelan.

RECOMMENDED HEALTH PROCEDURES

WORMING:

Horses one year or older--Treatment for all worms every six to eight weeks.

Foals--First worming at two-three months. Repeat at two month intervals.

Broodmares--De-worm every two months and within 24 hours after foaling.

VACCINATION:

Tetanus Antitoxin--Duration of protection not more than 10 days. To be given following injury to an animal that has not received tetanus toxoid. Foal should receive soon after birth.

Tetanus Toxoid--Duration of protection at least one year. Two injections 30 to 60 days apart. Booster given yearly.

Encephalomyelitis--(Sleeping sickness) Duration of protection for season of infection. Two injections about a month apart, usually given in spring prior to mosquito season.

Potomac Horse Fever--Primary protection requires two vaccinations about a month apart. Booster shot should be given annually, or immediately if an epidemic reported in area.

Influenza--Primary protection requires two vaccinations about a month apart. The horse should receive boosters four times a year if subject to heavy exposure, such as race and show horses or horses at public stables.

Rhinopneumonitis--Primary protection requires two vaccinations about a month apart. Booster should be given four times a year in areas of heavy exposure. Broodmares need boosters at five, seven and nine months of pregnancy for the virus strain which causes abortion.

Strangles--Primary protection requires two vaccinations about a month apart. Booster should be given annually or immediately if epidemic is reported.

Other vaccinations used occasionally--Venezuelan Equine Encephalomyelitis, Equine Viral Arteritis, Botulism, Rabies.

Dr. Alice makes two suggestions: Begin vaccinations when foals are about four to six months old, and work out a vaccination program with your local veterinarian who can advise you on the kind and degree of exposure.

HORSES NEED EXERCISE

Exercise is defined as "active use to give practice and training or to cause improvement."

It can also be described as "getting out and moving about; kicking up your heels."

Most horses don't get enough exercise.

How do we know that?

We know because studies indicate too many of our horses are too fat, and too many have nasty stall vices, and too many have too many injuries that are associated with poor physical condition.

If they are getting too little, how much is enough?

I often ask this question, but I seldom get a very satisfactory answer.

We know horses in the wild will move an average of 30 miles per day just looking for food, water and a good place to snooze. But what we don't really know is what constitutes enough exercise for a domesticated horse.

One renowned expert devotes a whole paragraph to exercise in his complete encyclopedia on horses. He says horses should exercise as much as possible on pasture. If

no pasture is available, exercise mature animals for an
hour or two a day under saddle or in harness.

Thanks much, but that just doesn't get it.

Obviously, different amounts of exercise are correct
for different horses--age, sex, health must be considered.
Young horses don't need the same type of exercise as an
older jumper.

A medical expert advises a horse's daily exercise
should consist of enough work to make the horse's pulse,
respiration and perspiration output increase to the point
where at least one of the three is noticeable.

That's not good enough either. If we follow that
guide, all we know for sure is that exertion has taken
place.

I think we have to go back to the definition of
exercise: "active use to give practice and training or to
cause improvement."

A young horse in a round pen or on a longe line will
show improvement in gait, pace, stopping ability or just in
paying attention, in about the same time he's had enough
exercise to rid himself of all his excess energy. It won't be
coincidental that his pulse and respiration are elevated or
that he's just started to break into a sweat on his neck.

An older horse in training will need a few minutes
just to warm up. So the rule of "walk the first mile out"
might be a good guide for starters Then we can go to work
on the performance lessons, past and present.

Using the definition of exercise, we'll know the horse
has had enough about the time he starts to show
improvement in his work. Just to make sure he has had
enough exercise, we can "walk him the last mile back."

There is another type of exercise every horse needs.
Every horse should have some time alone, free to roam.
Turn him out in a paddock or a pasture, or even a training

ring. Be sure he's got enough room to run, stop, turn, kick up his heels and get the kinks out.

Once a week, or once a month, you'll find the free exercise period will refresh the horse's mind.

If you aren't going to turn him out, or lunge him, or ride him, then at least get him walked every day.

Hand walking a horse isn't much fun, so hot walkers are dandy. A young horse should have at least a half hour on a hot walker if he is to get no other exercise that day. A mature horse being worked four of five days a week will need an hour daily on a hot walker when not worked.

The amount of work a horse received used to be measured in hours. A light work was from one to three hours, a heavy work from four to eight hours. (That measurement most often meant pulling a plow.) But time alone doesn't measure the true relationship between exercise and the horse's present physical condition.

Active use to give practice to an individual horse's skills or to cause improvement of those skills is a darn good guide to how much exercise is the right amount for that horse.

And if your riding skills aren't improving every day, *you* need a little more exercise.

STARTING YOUNG HORSES IS A SNAP

Two rules make the saddle training of young horses a snap.

Rule 1: Take it slow.

Rule 2: Never get a young horse hot.

Sounds too easy. Well, it's not too easy, but it is easy.

It doesn't matter what goal you have in mind for the young horse. The rules apply to race horses, western pleasure horses or dressage horses. Well-started horses do better in the beginning and they do better in the end. If you want a great performance from any horse, you can't beat a solid foundation.

I like to start all horses on the lunge line. It may take 10 to 15 days to get the young horse to work in both directions at all three gaits and stop on verbal command. But by going slowly, we progress rapidly. Never work the youngster until he is sweaty hot and breathing hard. The idea is to communicate your requests and have the horse understand and respond. Exercise is the least important factor at this point.

Always groom the baby, pick up his feet, and begin to teach him to tie before going to the arena for lunge work.

When the baby lunges well, and is totally relaxed during the grooming process, begin introducing him to his equipment. I take the equipment to the youngster's stall, let him see it, smell it and even taste it if he wants. The first few days I don't cinch the saddle and I don't have reins on the bridle. When the baby has accepted the equipment, I tack him and leave him in the stall for 15 to 20 minutes. Be sure someone keeps an eye on the baby so he doesn't get into any trouble while learning to accept his new burden.

With the horse lungeing well and carrying his equipment, I take him back to his stall after his arena work and I start slapping the saddle, tugging on the reins and generally putting weight in the stirrups. Usually you can step up on a completely relaxed horse within five to six days. Don't try to ride the horse until you've sat on him for three or four minutes three or four days in a row.

If you have had no difficulties, haven't rushed and haven't gotten the horse overheated, you should have a nice grooming session, followed by some lunge line work (while tacked) and then a few riding steps in the stall. Turn the horse and have him take a few steps, then stop him. Turn the other direction, walk and stop. With five days of practice, you should be able to ride the horse in his stall at the walk, turning and stopping. The horse should be accepting his work in a quiet manner.

Without rushing any of the young horse's work, he should be ready to ride out of the stall and into the arena about 30 days after you began his training. I walk in circles and in straight lines, stopping and turning for three or four days. I ask only that the horse remain relaxed and responsive to the verbal and leg cues. If there have been no problems, the horse will be ready to trot within five days; he may even start on his own. Walking, trotting, turning and stopping for the next 15 days will have the young horse ready for the canter, if he hasn't already tried it on his own.

If you have followed both rules, both you and the youngster should be very happy about the results to this point. The horse should never have been asked to do something in such a hurry that he became confused or frightened.

And he should never have been asked to work so hard he became overheated or out of breath.

There can be no learning without confrontation. That is a basic of horse training. So I understand the young horse will have to be disciplined on occasion, and I encourage it. A request followed by wrong action requires discipline. A request followed by a correct action requires praise.

Make it a rule to find a way to get many, many correct responses and reward them with plenty of praise. Accentuate the positive with praise. Eliminate a need for discipline by avoiding situations in which the horse might respond incorrectly.

Once the youngster gets 15 days of walking, trotting, cantering, turning and stopping experience, you will see how fast a horse can progress if you have taken the work slowly.

A young horse which has never been physically overtaxed is a happy horse, and a happy horse learns more quickly. A horse which has benefited from a slow progression of easy-to-understand lessons can handle the rapid introduction of new requests.

Baby steps for baby horses is the rule during the first 60 days.

Giant steps in understanding and performance ability begin to be the rule in the next 60 days.

Go slow if you want a horse to reach his future potential in a hurry.

A horse cool in training is hot in competition.

It's easy; it's just not too easy.

CURB OR SNAFFLE?

Believe me, bits are simple.

There are only two kinds. (There are plenty of variations.)

Neither kind of bit can work miracles.

Both kinds can be used to inflict pain, which is primarily what they were designed to do. At the same time, most advertisements today attempt to convince possible buyers the bit will solve training problems and never cause the horse any discomfort. Impossible! Bits don't solve training problems. And while they may not be causing discomfort, the best a bit can do is be comfortable.

Ask most horsemen and you'll be surprised to discover few know much about bits. Few can give an accurate definition of either kind of bit. And worst of all, few know how the bit they are using actually works.

I consider a snaffle a bit. (Lots of the world says a snaffle is a snaffle and a curb is a bit.)

I consider a curb a bit.

And that is it.

There is a snaffle and there is a curb. What's the difference? A snaffle has the reins attached opposite the mouthpiece and has no curb action and no poll action. A curb has both curb and poll action and has the reins attached below the mouthpiece so the principle of the lever and fulcrum is in effect.

Notice I did not mention the type of mouthpiece in either bit. That is because the type of mouthpiece does not define the bit. (You constantly hear that a snaffle is a bit with a jointed mouthpiece. Not true. A snaffle can have any type of mouthpiece you desire.)

A snaffle--with any kind of mouthpiece--requires the use of two hands on the reins in order for it to function efficiently. While the rider holds one rein steady, the other rein is bumped, thus causing the mouthpiece to press against the bar of the mouth on one side. The bit pressure causes discomfort and the horse gives in order to avoid the irritation.

You can come up with all the humane sounding jabberwacky you want, but the truth is the truth. Bits function on the theory the horse complies to avoid pain.

A lever action of the shanks of the curb move around the fulcrum (mouthpiece) and create pressure in the chin groove and at the poll. In addition, depending on the mouthpiece, pressures are applied to the tongue, the bars, and possibly the roof of the mouth.

Bits were invented about 1,000 B.C., starting out as a thong through the mouth or around the lower jaw. The idea was to inflict enough pain that the horse would comply with the handler's desire rather than put up with continued discomfort.

As technology advanced, bits became much more severe and painful, especially with the advent of the martingale, which allowed horsemen to apply great downward pressure to mouthpieces, which were discs, spikes and chains.

The Greeks were using such torture devices, as well as a version of the modern roller bit, as long ago as 500 B.C.

It is interesting to note that not much has changed in bits since that time. As soon as someone devised a different bit, with more or less painful possibilities, horsemen rushed to employ it. It is the same today. Horsemen seem to love the idea of a bit of any kind which will solve their particular training problem. Unfortunately, seldom does the horseman actually take the time to understand the bit he or she is using.

"I was told it was mild. I was told it is a good training bit. I was told a jointed mouthpiece is an easy bit." Don't accept what you are told. Accept your responsibility to learn the truth.

Learn the truth of these facts: "Cowboy snaffles" are extreme pain producers. No one using a mechanical hackamore actually knows how much pressure is being applied to the horse's jaw. The Tom Thumb is not constructed to be gentle; its loose shanks work like a crushing vise.

But then, I can't blame the bit.

Bits were designed to create discomfort, and I understand it, and I employ the principle that the horse will, when he comprehends, comply to avoid pain.

I also understand and endorse the fact that it is the horseman, not the bit, who inflicts the pain, or asks gently with a controlled pressure.

Xenophon, the first to write a complete book on horsemanship, recognized what he was using--spikes, discs and chains in the mouth--and how they should be used.

According to Xenophon, the key to the horse's acceptance of the bit is the "light hand."

Xenophon's observation was made 400 B.C. and was as true then as it is today. It is not so much how severe the bit, but how light the hand.

When it comes to mouthpieces, those most kind are the large, smooth, copper type. Ports help keep the horse from getting his tongue over the mouthpiece, and rollers and crickets sometimes soothe a nervous horse. All other mouthpieces are questionable. They may be of more importance to the condition of the rider than the horse.

Young horses do very well on the jointed mouthpiece snaffle. But they also do well on a snaffle with a small port, or a curved hollow rubber bar. The most important thing about the snaffle is the one holding the reins.

Older horses on curbs will respond to one-hand reining because the curb applies additional pressures which create a greater awareness of the rider's requests. But the most important part of the curb is the one holding the reins.

The full bridle is actually two bits, four reins. The full bridle is a snaffle, often called a Bridoon, and a curb used together. The most important part of the full bridle is the one holding the reins.

Any claim that a bit will solve training problems, reduce resistance, give more comfort, control the rogue, or get the horse to swim on his back while whistling Dixie is bunk.

Bits do nothing. Horsemen use bits.

Good horsemen learn how they work and why, then use them in the least abusive way possible.

IT FEELS GOOD TO HIM!

Grooming a horse is hard work.

To do the grooming job properly, you'll need a mane and tail comb, a metal curry comb, a rubber brush, a stiff brush, a soft brush and a hoof pick.

For perfection grooming--the kind that brings blue ribbons--you'll also need, although not necessarily for daily use, a pair of small electric clippers and a pair of large electric clippers, shampoo, a water scraper, soft rags and a bottle of baby oil. You should also have a hood, blanket and tail wrap.

Wow! It takes a lot of equipment.

Daily grooming is done just prior to working the horse. This grooming consists of removing mud and long hair with the metal curry comb, a quick rub with the rubber brush, a brief rub with the stiff brush (sometimes called a rice straw brush), and a once-over-lightly with the soft brush.

Use the mane and tail comb to remove tangles. Do the forelock as well as the mane and tail.

Do not use anything but the soft brush or a clean cloth on the horse's face.

Do not use the metal curry or the rubber brush below the knees or hocks.

Make sure you brush behind the fetlock joint and on the outside of the ears.

Always clean the horse's feet with the hoof pick before and after asking the horse for work.

The metal curry is used in a scraping manner, going in the direction of the hair.

The rubber brush is used by rubbing it in small circles, and the soft and stiff brushes always travel in the direction of the hair.

During the brushing phase of grooming, look for cuts, scrapes or nicks on the horse. If you find any, apply an antiseptic dressing. Also check carefully for any hock sores or nicks around the coronet band and dress them.

Make it an unbreakable rule never to put your horse away dirty. I don't recommend baths with soap or shampoos, as soap coats the hair, something not heathy for the horse. The horse is the only hairy animal which sweats, and he wants his hair to separate so his skin can breathe. Frequent baths with clear, cool water are beneficial and appreciated by your horse.

If you have not rinsed or bathed your horse after you have worked him, then you'll need to use lots of elbow grease and take plenty of time for the second phase of your daily grooming program.

Start with the rubber brush and give your horse a good rubdown. He likes it and it's good exercise for you. It also brings the dirt to the surface and removes most of the loose hairs.

A careful brushing with the stiff brush follows. Make sure you brush the horse thoroughly, including the hard-to-reach spots between the front legs, inside the back legs and under the chin.

A complete going-over with the soft brush comes next. Be sure to do the face and ears with this brush.

I prefer taking care of the mane and tail a little at a time rather than having to do the job all at once. This seems an easier way for both you and the horse. Let's start with the mane.

Never use scissors. Always "pull" the mane, tail and forelock in this manner: Take hold of a small section of the mane. Hold onto the long hairs to be pulled and back comb the remaining hairs out of the way. Wrap the long hairs you are holding around the comb and pull out with a sharp jerk. Repeat until you have removed the long hairs from the entire mane.

The length of the mane is generally determined by the breed and by what is most acceptable in your part of the county.

When you pull the horse's tail, begin with the top of the tail and jerk the short underneath hairs out. Short hairs sticking out make the tail look unkempt. You can keep a tail wrap on a horse that has an exceptionally bad tail or on a horse that rubs his tail.

The tail is considered short when it reaches only to the horse's hocks. But remember, when a horse is standing still, the tail should reach a little below the hocks because the horse will hold his tail out from his body while he is moving, making the tail look ever shorter than it really is.

It is absurd to have a horse's tail dragging the ground. In my opinion, not only does it look silly, (because it is unnatural), but it also indicates the handler of the horse is more interested in appearances than the welfare of the horse.

To get the tail to the desired length, simply tie a knot in the tail where you want it to end. Then pull out those hairs that hang below the knot. If the tail is not thick enough to suit you, many breeds now allow the supplementation of the tail. (In my opinion, a phony tail is used by phony people.)

The forelock is left heavy on certain breeds and in some parts of the country. Personally, I prefer a thin forelock that is not too long. You can thin and shorten the forelock the same as you do the mane.

It is a good idea to keep your horse blanketed.

A heavy blanket worn in the winter will keep the horse's hair smooth, and a day sheet worn in the summer keeps the hairs from being bleached by the sun. Winter coats are a reaction to the length of daylight. If you keep your horse "under the lights", you'll keep him from having a heavy, long winter coat. If you do blanket your horse, always remember to give him a few hours in the sun each day without the blanket, as horses absorb vitamins from the sun through their skin. If you live in a severely cold climate, you may want to add a hood and neck wrap. (How a blanket should fit will be discussed later.)

About a week before showing a horse, get out the electric clippers

Using the large clippers, start with the front legs, left side. Face the rear of the horse. Pick up the leg, holding it in your left hand. The palm of your hand should be on the cannon bone just above the fetlock joint. The foot will then hang down a little bit, permitting you to clip the back of the pastern and the back of the coronet band easily. Run the clippers against the hair from the coronet band to the fetlock joint. Do not clip against the hair above the fetlock joint except around the ergot.

When the back of the pastern is done, move the leg out in front of the horse and turn around so you now face in the same direction as the horse. Rest his leg on your right knee and clip the pastern from the coronet band to the fetlock joint.

Now set the foot down and clip from the knee down to the fetlock joint by running the clippers with the hair down the cannon bone. Clip behind the knee in the same way.

The rear legs are clipped in the same manner as the front legs.

However, you will find it harder to get to the back of the pastern on the rear legs. Sometimes it is easier to clip the back of the pastern if the horse is standing with his rear feet squarely under him.

Before clipping the bridle path--removal of the mane at the poll--with the large clippers, decide how long you want it to be. A fairly long bridle path helps make the horse appear to have a narrow throat latch and a longer neck. A short bridle path does just the opposite.

Start clipping the bridle path at the farthest point down the neck and clip up the neck to the poll. Make the first cut on an angle as this makes the mane lie over and look better. Be careful you do not cut into the forelock.

Use the large clippers under the horse's chin and to remove the long hairs at the throat latch. The small clippers are used around the muzzle, in the ears, and to remove the long hairs that grow just under and above the eyes.

You will find most horses rather resent having the hair in the ears clipped. Therefore, it's a good idea to start by trying to clip the ears without using any form of restraint on the animal. If the horse will not cooperate, then go to the lip chain or a twitch. (It is always best if you practice with the horse long before it is necessary to get the job done.)

Do not tie your horse while you are clipping him. Have someone hold him or simply leave him ground tied.

If weather permits, you may give your horse a bath a day or two before the show.

If you elect to use a shampoo, first give the horse a thorough rubdown with the rubber brush. Wet your horse all over before applying the shampoo and be careful you do not get shampoo in his ears, eyes or nostrils. Shampoo the entire horse.

You do not want to leave any soap on the horse's skin so make sure you rinse him thoroughly. Use clear, lukewarm water and do the job carefully and completely. Make sure you wash and rinse the horse well between and behind the back legs.

The mane and tail can be washed with horse or human shampoo, or you may prefer to use a special mane and tail shampoo. There are also special soaps with bleach to make your horse's white markings brighter.

After you have rinsed the horse thoroughly, use the water scraper to remove the excess water. Pay particular attention to the area under his belly as this is where the water collects.

Take your horse to a shaded area to let him dry. If he stands in the sun to dry, the sun makes the ends of the hair curl.

When he is dry, use the stiff brush as your first grooming tool, following it with the soft brush. Brush the horse completely with both brushes.

If you decided to use a coat dressing, try a soft cloth dampened with baby oil. There are some prepared coat dressings which come in spray cans, but you must rub these dressings in if you want them to do a really good job. Rub the cloth with the baby oil or coat dressing all over the horse, including his mane, tail and fetlock.

When you have finished this task, blanket your horse and keep him blanketed until show time. The blanket keeps the hair in place and helps the coat retain the natural oils. If you horse has white socks, it's a good idea to wrap his legs.

When show day arrives, you'll go through the entire grooming program again.

Just before you enter the show ring, you'll want to apply baby oil around the horse's eyes. This makes the eyes look larger and brighter. Also put baby oil around the muzzle as this brings out the color and gives the head much more appeal.

Rub your horse down lightly with a soft rag between classes. The rag, treated with a little baby oil, picks up the dust from his coat and has him shining for the next class.

7
A PLACE TO HANG A HALTER

A horse's house is his home.

And he really gets attached to it.

While there are a lot of slobs around who will live in a sloppy house, a horse won't--if he has a choice.

Horses are basically pretty neat and tidy.

When they get a neatness problem, it's often circumstantial. Horses will make a wet spot in a small corral or box stall because they urinate in the same place. The horse's idea of using the same spot all the time is a good one. The builder's idea of not using an absorbent base material is a bad one.

Pipe corrals that measure 12 by 12 feet or 12 by 24 feet are becoming very popular--with horseowners, not necessarily with horses. From a horse's point of view, they are too small, hard to keep clean, often don't give protection from the sun and rain and frequently are dangerously constructed.

If a horse is to live in a small corral, plan on providing him with plenty of exercise. Keep the corral raked daily. Wet spots need new soil and bedding daily.

A pipe corral should have some type of roofing, at least over half of it. Horses should not be left to bake in the summer sun or stand in the rain for days on end.

Hot sun can burn and it makes the ground hard and dry. Rain is not so bad, as far as the horse is concerned;

it's the mud of a small corral that's bad.

Pipe corrals get terribly muddy and mucky. It's virtually impossible to keep them dry. But extra soil can been added to the area under the roofing before it rains.

Once the rains start, the area under the roofing can be improved by the additions of sand or shavings.

Water buckets and automatic waterers should be placed so they are shaded at least part of the day, yet are not directly adjacent to the manger. Water and waste hay draw flies; but even worse, in combination they produce mold and become toxic.

Many pipe corrals are poorly constructed. They have nuts and bolts and sharp edges in all the places that horses like to stick their ears, noses and eyes. The consequences can be tragic, and the veterinarian's bills can be a lot higher than the initial investment in a good pipe corral.

A good pasture makes a great house for a horse.

But it's got to be a good pasture. Many aren't.

A good pasture has shelter, maybe natural, maybe man-made. A big tree is terrific.

A good pasture has plenty of fresh water, doesn't flood badly, has some high spots and is free of dangerous obstacles and noxious weeds. A good pasture is one which is well-fenced.

It is not necessary for a good pasture to provide the horse with food. The owners of the horse should know the nutritional value of the pasture and take appropriate action.

Barns and box stalls can be palaces or dungeons.

Good box stalls are in good repair. That means the walls haven't been chewed in half and left that way. That means there aren't nails and eyebolts sticking out of every wall. That means the door closes without falling off the hinges.

To be a palace, a box stall must have good light and good ventilation. It should be cool in the summer, warm in the winter and dry when it rains.

A good stall affords a view. No horse should be stuck behind bars so he can't see what is going on around him.

If a horse sweats or freezes or can't see the activity around him, then his barn or box stall is "solitary confinement." That's not an easy sentence.

And if a box stall or barn isn't cleaned and rebedded daily, if the flooring isn't freshened weekly, if the construction isn't safe, the horse that lives in that house isn't going to be happy.

Deep down inside, every horse likes a neat, clean, tidy fresh castle. It makes him feel proud when his friends come to visit.

WHAT YOU NEED AROUND THE BARN

There are certain necessities which make a house a home.

For example, every horse needs a good supply of water. Automatic waterers are great if they are kept clean and in perfect repair. That means they must be checked and cleaned daily. If you choose water buckets, they must be cleaned daily and refilled at least twice per day--more often on very hot days.

Feeding in a good manger is the best idea, but in a box stalled bedded with straw or shavings, hay can be fed on the ground. Grain should be fed in a bucket. Do not use hay nets. If placed high, hay falls into the horse's eyes, the best of the hay falls to the ground and the horse doesn't eat with his head down as he was designed to do. If placed low, the horse can get a foot caught in the net. Horses also often tear off and swallow nylon strings which are not digestible.

Equipment you'll need around the barn includes double-ended snaps, brass or nickel, a manure fork or a pitch fork, depending on the bedding you use, wall hooks for buckets, rubber-covered chains or stall guards so the solid doors can be left open and a solid, large wheelbarrow.

You may also want a grass rake, a barn broom, a leather punch, hammer, screweyes, long water hose, tack bar for towels or blankets, sponges and oil-based cleaner for tack and germicidal stable wash/disinfectant.

FIGHT THE GOOD FIGHT

The horse fly problem seems to be worse than ever every year. At least, it seems that way.

Nothing you can do will be completely effective, but there are some steps you can take to make life a little more bearable for your horse and a lot less pleasant for the flies.

First, eliminate fly breeding areas, such as piles of damp hay and manure and muddy areas around water containers. (You've probably been told it is okay to have a big muddy spot around a water trough so the horse's feet will get plenty of moisture when he gets a drink. Bad idea. Getting the horse's feet wet, then having them dry out again in a matter of minutes, is damaging, not beneficial. There are better ways to care for your horse's feet.)

Second, use a wipe type fly repellent consistently in the morning and afternoon. I've found fly sprays more expensive and less effective, since much of the repellent ends up in the air rather than on the horse. Fly sprays don't often work well. Neither do fly wipes, unless you change brands every two weeks. Both, however, do some good for short periods of time. And making the effort to help the horse seems to make me feel better.

Don't get crazy. If a little is good, a lot isn't necessarily better. If you put too much repellent on a horse, it can cause tiny sores and the horse may suffer patchy hair loss, especially around the face.

You can try brewer's yeast. Feed two tablespoons to each horse every two or three days. After about 30 days, your horse should not be bothered by flies.

But brewer's yeast doesn't always work.

So you can try apple cider vinegar. Give each horse a half a cup of apple cider vinegar each day. Your horse should not be bothered by flies after about two weeks.

But vinegar doesn't always work.

You can try fly predators. Dr. Alice buys them every year and it makes her happy. (I've never seen a single fly predator eat a single fly. Don't tell Dr. Alice.)

But fly predators don't always help.

You can try fly bait. You sprinkle it on the ground around stall doors or near waterers. Be sure your dogs or cats don't eat the bait. You'll see lots of dead flies wherever you put the bait, so you have proof positive you are accomplishing something.

But fly baits don't eliminate the problem, or even seem to reduce it significantly.

You can try fly traps. The thing I like about them is that they fill up with dead flies and I can say, "See how fewer flies there are," as I shoo the flies away from my horse's face.

You can put sticky creams around the horse's eyes. Try not to get the stuff in his eyes. The appearance of the cream will satisfy your need to do something.

But sticky creams don't often work.

Here's a suggestion: If you have a stall, close the doors and shade the windows and hang a eucalyptus branch inside. This method seems to work best if the horse gets a lot of work before he is closed in the stall. Otherwise, he eats the branch and tears down the window shades and lets in a lot of flies.

You can't win!

But you can fight the good fight, and a fly swatter helps!

HOT DAYS ARE HARD

Hot, hot, hot, hot!
Long, hot summer days are just as hard on horses as they are on you. Maybe harder.

Preparing for summer heat is necessary if the horse is going to survive. And since the horse can't pick up a hammock, a sunshade and a lemonade at the local hardware store, it's up to you.

A little additional thought and an extra few minutes of time will do the trick.

With the first heat wave, the horse's daily diet should undergo a change, just as yours does. You eat a lot more salads, cold cuts and easy-to-fix dinners. The horse, however, just wants less hot foods. Cut out the concentrates--grains and supplements, and substitute some extra hay, or pellets or hay cubes.

When the heat arrives, you don't dress the same. Bikinis don't suit horses, but a reduction in weight does. Get the horse's weight down and he'll feel a lot better during the summer.

We perspire when it's hot, and the horse sweats. In both cases there is a salt loss. The horse needs more salt during the summer months, and it's easy to give him plenty. (More about salt in the next section.)

Finally, make sure your horse is prepared for summer by being sure the water supply is adequate and functional.

Some horses will drink 30 gallons or more of water a day during the summer. The water bucket must be large enough and filled often enough to quench that kind of thirst.

If you use automatic waterers, great! But be sure they are working and are not in the direct sun, as the water can get so hot the horse won't drink it.

Summer riding, of course, is a lot of fun when both parties can enjoy it.

Ride in the early morning or in the evening when it is cooler. Don't ride during the hottest part of the day. And keep in mind that you may be able to take the sun, but you aren't doing all the work. (If you don't want to pick up a 25-pound sack of grain and run around with it, the horse probably doesn't want to haul you around either.)

Warm the horse up before you start a ride. That may sound silly on a hot day, but it should be done. A warm-up period for the horse accelerates his breathing, which raises the oxygen level in the blood. The horse needs a good oxygen level to work well, especially in the heat.

When riding in the heat, your horse will sweat. Sweating is his way of expelling heat. (Horses are the only hairy animals which sweat.) However, if the horse gets too hot, he'll stop sweating or his breathing will become very rapid. Rapid breathing is an attempt to fill his lungs with cool air to reduce body temperature. Unfortunately, rapid breathing doesn't work as a horse cannot pant like a dog.

A horse that is overheated should be walked out until cool and given small amounts of cool water periodically. Don't let the horse drink as much cold water as he wants at one time. If the horse appears dehydrated, or so tired he won't walk, call a veterinarian immediately.

If the horse has had a good ride, and is just sweating, give him a nice cool, clear water bath, a drink every now and then, and walk him until he is dry. Put him away with a friendly pat.

There will be days so hot you won't want to do any riding. Neither will the horse. On those days, make yourself and your horse as comfortable as possible. On other days, you'll both be hot to trot.

MORE ABOUT SALT

As you sit around the pool, sipping iced tea and catching a few rays to improve that summer tan, think about your horse and say, "Salt."

The salt block you put in the manger last summer and the salt contained in the prepared grain mix you feed may not be sufficient.

As the temperature and humidity climb, you perspire and your horse sweats. It's the body's way of reducing heat buildup. The more the sweat loss, the greater the need for salt and trace mineral replacement.

The average horse needs 50 to 60 grams of salt per day. On a warm day, a horse may easily lose that much salt through sweating and urination. If he is worked moderately, he will lose even more.

To replace that amount of lost salt, the horse will have to have about a four-ounce intake of salt, according to the U.S. National Research Council. (You'll have to make your own determination about your horse's salt need by observing his behavior and condition.)

Salt and trace minerals play a very important role in keeping the horse healthy. And a big loss of salt through sweating can lead to many observable changes in your horse.

A horse deficient in salt and trace minerals usually shows it through physical and behavioral reactions.

Chewing on fences or mangers and eating dirt are behavioral changes.

Physical reactions can be noted in weight losses, rough coat and listless eyes. In addition, the horse may exhibit fatigue when worked.

Significant loss of electrolytes (salts dissolved in body fluids) also can lead to excessive fatigue, muscle spasms and cramps, dehydration and exhaustion. These conditions are normally seen during stress situations, but also can result from moderate work during very hot weather.

The amount of salt contained in hay and grain may be fine during the winter, but may not be sufficient during the summer.

Since most prepared grain mixes list salt and trace minerals as ingredients (but don't tell you how much), you can't rely on them to provide enough salt.

So it's to the horse's benefit if you have salt constantly available in loose-salt form. Loose salt, just tossed in his manger, is easier for the horse to eat than block salt. Unlike cattle, the horse has a smooth tongue, so he cannot easily get enough salt by licking a block.

When a horse is in desperate need of salt, he will sometimes chew off big hunks from a salt block, or consume the whole thing. This can cause a colic condition.

Iodized salt, or the red blocks, are not usually as well-liked by horses as the white blocks.

Do not salt a horse once a week, a practice that is fairly common but incorrect. A horse cannot store salt in his system so he'll be oversupplied one day, short the next.

Salt serves the horse in a number of ways. It stimulates the secretion of saliva, making food more palatable and aiding in digestion.

As a nutrient, it provides sodium and chlorine, which are necessary to establish and maintain the correct electrolyte balance.

A horse that is getting enough salt each day will enjoy better health and will have greater endurance.

WHEN WINTER WINDS BLOW

Tramping through mud in a cold, cutting rain isn't fun, but it's a fact of life when winter winds blow.

For man, it's pretty easy to get out of the rain. But for too many horses, it's impossible.

Luckily, horses are pretty hardy creatures and usually aren't affected much by cold rains or even snow storms if they have the opportunity to move around and find nature's shelters.

Most horses have winter weather problems when they are "protected" by man. (It's often all too easy to say, "He'll be all right," as you sit in front of the fire.)

If kept in a small pen or pasture, a lot of horses aren't going to be all right, unless they get a little help from their friends.

Without some attention, thousands of horses will suffer mud fever, cracked heels, rain scald or thrush this winter.

Mud fever is a condition which results from the horse standing in constant dampness for prolonged periods, such as being fetlock deep in corral mud for several days. It can even occur when a horse stands in a stall bedded by damp wood shavings, says Dr. Alice.

The moisture on the lower legs weakens the skin, which is irritated by the mud and dirt. Eventually, the skin cracks and is attacked by bacterial or fungal infections. Mud fever can even occur on the upper legs and belly if the horse must lie down in the mud.

Cracked heels is a similar problem normally seen in the groove at the back of the hoof between the bulbs of the heels. Infections here exude serum and pus commonly called "grease," explains Dr. Alice.

Rain scald is most often seen on the rump and back. It is an infection similar to mud fever caused by constant dampness and then chapping of the skin.

Thrush attacks the frog and sole of the foot, and is again associated with constant dampness, plus mud or dirt.

All of these conditions can be extremely painful, can result in lameness, and are preventable with a little effort on the part of the horse owner.

It is not a good idea to shave the hair from the legs of any horse which will be standing in a small, exposed corral or pasture. The hair on the legs is a good protection, and should be left.

If the horse is going to be out in the elements this winter, some type of overhead protection is needed. The shelter need not be elaborate or fancy, but it must provide the horse the opportunity to remain fairly dry for periods of time.

Dry footing is a must.

The horse can run around in mud most of the time, but he needs a spot of high ground so his legs and feet can dry out from time to time. The area need not be big, it simply needs to be dry.

A windbreak--hedges, trees, canvas, wood fencing--is just fine as long as it gives the horse an opportunity to get away from a scalding, chapping wind.

Waterproof blankets are a big help for horses if someone checks the blanket for dampness daily. Rain often runs under a blanket, soaking the inside. A horse is much better off without a blanket than with a wet blanket.

To protect the legs from mud fever and cracked heels, the horse's legs should be washed clean, dried, and coated with Vaseline, lard or better still, a zinc and castor oil ointment. Any of these grease applications should be cleaned off every few days and reapplied to a clean dry leg.

The hooves can be protected by an application of a hoof dressing. Those which contain lanolin are especially effective, Dr. Alice says.

Finally, the horse which is going to be out needs a good balanced diet with an oily supplement, such as corn oil.

These minor efforts can help, but even with an ounce of prevention, total protection is not assured.

Check the horse daily.

If any of these winter ailments should appear, move the horse to a stall, clean the affected areas with lukewarm water and a mild antiseptic, then keep the horse dry.

FITTING THE BLANKET

Horses are constantly wearing clothes which are small, medium or large, which means their clothes are usually too small, just right or too big. Two out of three isn't good enough.

If you are going to get your horse a blanket, and you want it to fit, then you should measure your horse. To do it right, it takes two--one to hold the horse still, one to measure.

Start at the center of the horse's chest, and take the tape across the point of his shoulder along his side, ending in the middle of his tail. This measurement--76 or 78 inches, or whatever, will give you a good estimate for sizing.

When you get the blanket--if your measuring was any good at all--the blanket should be snug around the neck and the spine of the blanket should end at the top of the tail. Different styles of blankets have different side lengths. A stall blanket is shorter on the sides than a turnout blanket, which drops lower to afford greater protection from the elements.

In the front, a good fit has a good overlap, so there is no gap across the chest and it is snug around the neck.

Surcingles should be adjusted tight enough so you can barely get your hand sideways (about 4 inches) between the horse and the surcingle.

Leg straps should be adjusted in about the same way. You want them loose enough so the horse can walk and move comfortably, but not so loose he could get a foot caught in one. Crossing the leg straps at the center (between the horse's back legs) helps reduce the possibility of a foot getting caught. Always snap to the same side of the blanket as the strap originates.

JUST SNOOZING

Once you get your horse's housing needs taken care of and have prepared him for all seasons, what do you suppose he's going to spend his time doing?

Well, horses spend the second greatest portion of their lives resting. (Eating occupies the greatest portion, as if you didn't know.)

Horses rest in three distinct ways. They doze, they slumber and they deep sleep.

When dozing, horses all take on the same basic posture and expression. The neck is horizontal and relaxed; the lower lip droops a little; a greater percentage of their weight is on the forehand, and they bend one hock and rest the toe of the hoof.

Horses can doze anywhere and at any time. The horse doesn't fully rest when dozing. Although his front legs have a nifty anatomical structure that allows him to rest while standing (better than other animals), the muscles of his hind legs are not at full rest.

You will notice that every few minutes the horse will shift his weight and rest the opposite hind foot.

When dozing, horses seem to be completely unaware of what is going on, but they are not. A dozing horse can move very quickly, can kick with accuracy and can bolt. Few of us, and definitely no tigers, will ever catch a dozing horse unaware and off guard.

Since adult horses can rest quite well while standing, they lie down only when they feel completely safe. Many horses foaled and raised on small farms or ranches will lie down more frequently than horses that have been moved from place to place or were raised on a big ranch.

Backyard horses generally have little to fear and usually don't have well-developed herd instincts.

When a horse slumbers, he'll lie with both his front feet and hind feet under his body, and he'll usually bend his neck toward his feet, then rest his chin on the ground. If in a herd, slumbering horses will always have a standing horse on guard duty. The guard horse is not a special horse, just the one that didn't get down soon enough. The guard horse will remain on duty until one of the slumbering horses rises.

Even with horses raised in small pastures, the rule of guard duty applies. Surprisingly enough, it also remains true with horses in box stalls. You can check 20 box stalls at any time, day or night, and you'll never find all the horses slumbering. At least one stands guard duty.

In deep sleep, the horse lies on its side, usually with one front leg bent and both back legs stretched.

If you are very observant about horses' sleeping patterns, there is no need for a pregnancy test on mares, according to some authorities. Once pregnant, mares will not lie completely over on their sides in deep sleep, I've been told.

I have seen pregnant mares lie over completely on their sides. I can't say if they were deep sleeping or just resting. Personally, I like to see them have a foal, then I know they were pregnant.

Most horses awake quite quickly from any type of sleep. Once up from slumber or a deep sleep, they will stretch and yawn, loosen their muscles, and go about the day's business, which consists mostly of eating and dozing.

8
EVERY YEAR WE ALL GROW OLDER

Who's happy about January 1 being the official birthday for most registered horses?

Certainly not the new foal. Nor the mare. Nor the stallion. Nor the owners or exhibitors.

Then who?

The bookkeepers, that's who!

To make it convenient for record keepers, January 1 was established as the official birthday for horses by most breed registries, regardless of when the horse was foaled. And that means a young horse, whether six days, six weeks, or six months old, becomes one year old on the first of January following his birth. Thereafter, he leaps into a new age bracket with the passing of each calendar year.

Foals and mares don't like the January 1 birthday if they live in the northern hemisphere. (It's not so bad if you live in the southern hemisphere.) In the U.S., it's cold, wet, windy and snowy in January, and a very silly time to give birth.

It's not nice to fool Mother Nature, who knows it's best for horses to be born in the late spring, when the temperatures are warmer and the grass is greener.

Mother Nature shows her displeasure at man's attempts to force artificial early breeding seasons by giving the horse a low conception rate for winter breedings. (The rate, of course, goes up if the mare is artificially inseminated.) There is also a high mortality rate among winter newborns, even with our technological advances.

The best time for breeding mares, according to Dr. Alice, is mid-May to about the end of September. Foals would be born approximately 11 months, 10 days later, or anywhere from April to early September.

Studies done by Colorado State University have established the best breeding time for stallions is in June. Semen output is highest during the latter part of the established breeding season, and is double in July what it is in January.

But with January 1 being the official birthday, show and race horse owners (for that matter any owner of a competition horse) refuse to think of waiting to breed mares in July and August. They believe it is to their advantage to have a foal born as close as possible to January 1. The results of public sales would support their contention that early foals are more in demand and command higher prices than late foals. The idea, of course, is that early foals will be bigger, stronger, better-muscled and faster than those born later in the year, even though they are--on the record book--the same age.

And show judges seem to think the same way. They usually pick the largest and most mature-looking horses in classes featuring youngsters. In fact, it would be a subject of controversy if a judge picked a young horse over older stallions or mares in a grand champion halter class.

But Mother Nature may be fooling us all.

The records show that even though we are attempting to force an early birthday so we'll have more winners, it isn't working.

A study by the American Quarter Horses Association of winners of the All American Futurity during a 10-year period reveals one winner was foaled in January, two in February, three in March, one in April, two in May and one in June. The average birth date was March 27.

Two more random studies showed the average birth date of 73 American Quarter Horse Association champions to be March 28. And the average birth date of 829 Register of Merit winners was April 8. Sneaky Pete, who went to the Quarter Horse World Championships twice, and was the leading point earner in the state of California in western riding several different years, was foaled on September 10. He was a junior horse even when he was considered a senior horse.

Horses would be a lot happier if all this horse birthday stuff was moved to May 1. Let the bookkeepers enter that in their records.

THERE WILL BE MORE

It's breeding season again.

All the magazines have just published their Stallion editions, and all the advertisements are pleading with you to bring your mare to Hot Stuff or Super Duper or The Winner.

Well, I'm pleading with you not to breed your mare unless:

1. You know what you want.

Don't breed a mare just to get a foal because you think it would be nice. In the long and short run, breeding on that basis is a disaster.

The net results will include a financial loss for you and probably a pretty miserable life for the foal. Foals bred on this basis too often end up being a burden to the breeder, never are put to a useful life, and for the most part, are neglected.

Breed for a pleasure horse, or halter horse, or race horse, or a horse to sell. But know what it is you want.

And once you know what it is you want, study. Have a plan which will result in producing the kind of foal which can perform to your expectations, or to the standards of competition you plan to enter, or which will appeal to a large group of buyers. Don't leave things to chance.

Like begets like. It's not very often that two slow horses are going to produce one fast horse. Or that two poorly-conformed horses are going to produce a top halter prospect. You can't just breed a tall horse to a short horse in order to get a medium horse.

Only people not concerned with the welfare of horses breed anything to anything just to get a foal.

2. Don't breed your mare unless she's really worth breeding.

The difference between horsemen and dudes is obvious when you hear a person say, "Well, if she can't perform, we can always breed her."

Good horsemen don't breed mares that have proven they aren't good at what it is they are supposed to do.

If a mare can't run fast, or pleasure, or jump or halter, she isn't a good prospect for producing a fast runner, or pleasure horse, or jumper or halter horse, or whatever.

If a mare has poor conformation, don't expect her to produce great conformation. If she's predisposed to lameness, expect her foal to inherit her weakness.

The rule of breeding is breed the best to the best to get the best. If you breed less than the best, you'll get less than the best, and in that case, it is usually the resulting foal which suffers in the long run.

3. Don't breed your mare unless you can afford to breed to the best stallions.

There are too many bad stallions around. My guess is that 70 per cent of them would make nice geldings, and then there'd still be too many bad stallions. If a mare shouldn't be bred because she didn't measure up to a high standard, then you shouldn't breed to a stallion who doesn't measure up to a high standard.

Be sure you select a stallion on the basis of his blood and his accomplishments, not his service fee. Picking a stallion because his stud fee fits your budget is not good genetic selection.

So please, don't breed your mare unless you know what you want, know she's worth breeding and you can book to a great stallion.

Like begets like!

IF YOU ARE GOING TO BREED, STUDY GENETICS

What everyone wants is a champion.

What everyone gets is an opportunity to pay their money and take their chances.

Genetics, or the science of heredity, is supposed to be important to the horse breeder because, through its study, he should be able to produce a horse with the predictable inheritable traits he wants.

So let's make a quick study of genetics.

Horses have 64 chromosomes arranged in 32 pairs. Each chromosome carries many thousands of genes. These genes contain all the information about what the new horse will be.

Now if the genes would behave themselves, you might make a pretty accurate prediction about the new foal's inheritable traits, such as how fast he could run, his size, disposition, color, etc.

But genes are ornery little devils and they have what is called "variable expressivity." A simple example of variable expressivity is that all chestnut horses are not the same shade of chestnut. In other words, some of the genes express themselves a little differently.

Genes give the new foal two types of inheritance. The first is qualitative and the second is quantitative.

There are relatively few qualitative genes and lots of quantitative genes. Those which are quantitative are affected by the new foal's environment, and that becomes a problem. For example, there is a medium to high degree of inheritability in the speed of a horse. But the speed trait comes from quantitative genes and is therefore influenced by lifestyle, food, sunshine, training techniques, etc.

So to select the right stallion for your mare in the hope of getting a very fast foal, you need to know about the quantitative genes and environments of both parents.

The stallion many have average quantitative speed genes that got a whole lot of help from his environment. Or he may have had a lot of speed from genes that weren't helped at all by his environment.

The information you need is difficult to acquire, but you can do several things in order to find good breeding stock.

1. Compare the performance records of stallions. Don't worry about the pedigree of a horse further back than three generations, as the great-grandsire will have little influence on your foal.

2. Select from the very best bloodlines for the type of horse you want. You can ignore 90 per cent of the available stallions; they should have been gelded long ago.

3. Try to find a superior breeding animal, one with prepotency (homozygously dominant genes). How do you know if the horse has dominant genes? You'll have to check the record of his offspring for what you suspect are inheritable traits. Even then, it's just a guess.

Inbreeding, the mating of closely related animals, is a method of producing homozygously dominant horses.

However, inbreeding has its drawbacks and is not for the average horseowner. Inbred horses are sometimes just a little "loco."

Line breeding is a special form of inbreeding, which attempts to emphasize the influence of a single ancestor in the pedigree, and can be very helpful to the average horseowner.

Outbreeding is the mating of individuals not closely related in the last three or four generations, and is probably the best system for the breeder of fewer than 10 or 12 mares.

It is to be hoped our quick study of genetics has demonstrated the complexities of the subject and has you a bit confused as to the results you can expect.

Based on the confusion and complexities I have wrought, the laws of probability say my recommendations should not be followed by 87 per cent of readers. Consequently:

1. Select a broodmare and stallion which please you in both appearance and performance records.

2. Considering just the stallion and mare, breed the best performer to the best performer in your field of interest. That's the law of selectivity; it's also your best chance for good results.

3. Understand that the study of genetics proves "What you see ain't necessarily what you get."

4. Continue to study genetics so you can be as confused and unsure as the best experts, and maybe it'll result in the much-needed further study of horses.

DON'T BOIL WATER OR SPANK BOTTOMS!

It's foaling time. Ah, the joy of being a new parent, even if that funny, long-legged baby does have silly, crooked whiskers.

The birth of a foal is a beautiful and exciting experience, but there can be danger too.

Understanding the foaling process eliminates some of the dangers, while unskilled or untimely assistance increases the chances of disease or even death for the foal, the mare or both.

Dr. Alice suggests you do little to assist nature.

"Nature does a pretty good job on her own. And in too many cases, an overly-helpful owner creates problems where there were none."

Dr. Alice recommends you have three things on hand at foaling time:

1. A bottle of iodine.
2. Some clean towels.
3. A clean, dry sheltered area for the mare and foal.

The iodine is to be poured on the foal's navel cord just after the cord breaks. This is extremely important, since navel infection is very common among foals. The cord represents a direct passage to the foal's bladder and to the blood supply to the liver. Any infection that gets into this passage is transmitted to the rest of the foal's system and can easily result in "joint or navel ill," a severe disease that may cause death.

The clean towels are used to dry the foal after birth. It isn't necessary you do this, but especially in cold weather, drying the foal keeps it from being chilled and gets the little one's circulation going. This can also be considered part of the imprinting of the foal, a procedure Dr. Alice will address later.

If the weather is nice, the best place for the mare to foal is a grassy pasture. But if you want the mare sheltered, be sure to put her in your biggest stall. Both straw and wood shavings make good bedding.

Now that you're prepared, let's check the sequence of events.

The average pregnancy is 342 days, give or take 10 days. As foaling time approaches, look for telltale signs. The mare's milk glands will enlarge and a waxy substance may develop on the ends of the nipples. Milk may drip or stream from the nipples, a good indication foaling will occur within 15 minutes to 48 hours.

As the time nears, the mare will exhibit nervousness, showing all the signs of colic, for indeed she does have stomach cramps.

The water bag will appear and break. Don't be concerned; it's natural that there is a lot of water. In 15 minutes or less, the foal's front feet should appear. In a normal birth presentation, the foal's head will be between the front feet. It is not uncommon for the mare to get up and walk around before the birth is complete. From the time the feet first appear, it will take from two to 10 minutes for the remainder of the birth process.

Let a normal birth take place, Dr. Alice advises. Your main job as the observer is to look for signs of an abnormal birth presentation.

If anything other than two front feet and the head should appear, or if nothing appears after 15 minutes of hard labor, call your vet, describe exactly what you see and follow instructions carefully.

If the sack is still over the foal's head after the birth process is complete, stick your fingers through the membrane at the foal's mouth, then pull the sack back away from the nostrils so the foal can breathe. Don't do anything more until the mare has cleaned the foal and both are relaxed. Then pour the iodine on the foal's navel cord and rub the foal with the clean towels.

It will take from five minutes to three hours for the mare to expel all the afterbirth. Collect the afterbirth so it may be checked by your vet.

When the foal decides it's time for a drink, he'll try to get to his feet; this can take from 15 minutes to an hour. You'll want to ease his struggle, but don't. The exercise is good for the foal.

The foal should be nursing within two hours. If not, then a little assistance may be helpful. Don't try to push the foal toward the mare; the foal won't go. Stand on the opposite side of the mare from the foal and try to get the foal to suck on your fingers. Then guide the foal toward the milk. A little squirt on the nose will get the little squirt's attention.

The foal should pass the meconium from the rectum shortly after having a good drink of milk, says Dr. Alice. If the foal shows signs of straining, tail elevation or cramping, call your vet. Do not give the foal an enema yourself.

Within 12 hours of foaling, have your vet check both the mare and foal and administer disease-preventing medication to both.

As simple as it is, that's the wonderful miracle of foaling.

Oh, I almost forgot, you can check the sex of the foal while you are drying him/her off. That way you can call her her, or him him instead of "The Foal."

IMPRINTING IS EXCELLENT IDEA

Imprinting the foal is a fancy way of saying the foal learns to accept you and all the handling he'll get in the years to come. It is beneficial to both of you.

"It is so easy to accomplish when the foal is very young that it is foolish not to do it," says Dr. Alice. "There are two important things to remember. Be gentle and be consistent," she says.

Before you start imprinting, be sure both the mare and foal are completely relaxed, and that both are well rested from the birthing process.

You can start by rubbing the foal all over. Let the foal smell you, and then, of course, let him taste you. Put your fingers in his mouth and make sure he accepts you handling his tongue. Put your fingers in his ears, and touch his ears all over. Put your fingers in his nostrils. Do this until the foal shows no resistance and do all of this several times during every imprinting session.

Now go to the foal's legs. Rub your hands up and down his legs and pick up his feet. Slap the bottoms of his feet with your hands so he never thinks twice about having his feet handled for trimming or shoeing. Again, continue until the foal ignores your efforts.

Catch and handle the foal frequently during the first few days. If you catch him often enough with no traumatic experiences, he'll be very easy to approach. Once caught, repeat all the touching he already knows. Then add something new. For example, practice putting a halter on and then taking it off. You can begin to teach the foal to lead within five days.

The more you do--slow and easy--the more confident the foal will become and the better he or she will retain their early training.

Imprinting isn't a revolutionary idea. All handling of horses is imprinting. The great advantage of imprinting as it is being presented here is how easy it is for both the handler and the foal.

SOMEONE MUST BE A GOOD MAMMA

The chances are good that sooner or later you will be involved with the care of an orphaned foal or a foal whose mother is not producing enough milk.

Don't panic. The fact the foal's mother must be replaced is sad enough. Take a deep breath; get started. Caring for the new baby is actually easier than it appears at first.

Doing everything possible to keep the baby healthy should be your primary concern.

The first step, in sequence of importance, is to make certain the foal's navel cord stump has been well-saturated with iodine as soon as possible after foaling. This helps keep infection from entering the foal's system.

Your second step is to provide the foal with colostrum, providing the mother cannot do it. Colostrum is in the mare's first milk, that which is produced during the first 12 hours after foaling. The colostrum contains antibodies the mare has built up to protect the foal from disease.

If the mare dies before the foal gets the colostrum, it is strongly advised that another mare that has just foaled be found and milk be supplied by her. In most cases, this is virtually impossible and in my opinion, a time-consuming frustration. I recommend you call your veterinarian, who will administer antibiotics, serum containing antibodies, vitamins, and will give the baby an enema.

What will really make the foal happy and healthy is something eat.

There are commercially-produced milk replacers just for foals. These are probably your best bet. They are designed especially for this purpose and are readily available through local feed stores. Such milk replacers are relatively inexpensive and easy to use.

Then there are some mix-it-yourself formulas.

A little snack, which should be fed to the foal in a baby bottle six to eight times around the clock during the first 10 days, is prepared by using two pints of low-fat cow's milk (about three percent fat), a half-pint of warm water, one and one-half ounces of corn syrup, one to two ounces of limewater, two drops of cod liver oil and a pinch of bone flour. The ingredients are easy to find, with the possible exception of limewater, usually found at pharmacies. Limewater is a solution of slaked lime (lime that has had the chemical balance changed) used to counteract an acid condition. For foals, the acid condition would be known as colic.

A little simpler formula can be made by using one pint of low-fat cow's milk, four ounces of limewater, and two teaspoons of corn syrup. A half-pint of this formula should be fed every hour on the hour for the first four or five days. After that, increase the amount to a little more than a pint and feed every two hours.

Commercially-prepared milk replacers for human babies can be fed to orphaned foals, but they must be diluted with water by about half.

My preference is to find a fresh nanny goat--not too hard to do--stand her on a bale of hay and let her gradually assume the duties of motherhood. If you introduce the foal and goat to one another carefully every hour during the first day, both will usually get the idea and carry on naturally from there.

Mamma goat will jump onto the bale of hay each time the baby horse wants a snack, and you can go your merry way concentrating on other chores and anticipating a good night's sleep.

Also try the Internet. There are lots of "wet mare on loan" programs among major horses breeders, and you may find just what you need in your area. It's worth the effort.

One other tip about orphaned foals. The best place for them is out in the sunshine in a pasture where they can get plenty of healthy exercise.

And curb your motherly instincts. You'll find the orphaned foal is destined to be a spoiled brat without a great deal of assistance.

OUT ON HIS OWN

There comes a time in the life of every little girl and boy horse when it's necessary to say, "Good-bye, Mamma."

Weaning time is arriving earlier and earlier in the lives of lots of horses. Years ago it was common practice to leave a foal with the mare for at least six months. Today, most foals, under average conditions, are weaned at about four months. There are those who wean at three months, and even some halter-horse conditioners who recommend weaning as early as two months.

The idea of early weaning is that mares are not particularly good milk producers, so with our improved feeding and handling techniques, the babies will grow faster, be bigger and take on more of the look the show world or marketplace wants.

Personally, I don't like the idea of trying to create a look, when what is already there is, in it's way, already perfect.

Dr. Alice says it's not so much when you wean as how you do it. "Weaning must be done in the least stressful manner possible. And it must be done when both the mare and foal are healthy. Do not wean a baby which has any disease symptoms, such as a dirty nose or a cough."

I prefer to determine the time of weaning according to circumstances which have little to do with the foal's age. I shorten or lengthen the time the foal is with the mare based on the disposition and characteristics of the mare.

If I really like the disposition of the mare, I may leave the foal with her for a full four months or even a bit longer. If the mare is cranky, or has characteristics I don't like, I wean the foal as early as possible--maybe two months.

I'm a firm believer the foal will have more or less of the mare's traits depending on the length of time they are together.

I don't want a baby with a mare which is dominated by other mares; that behavior tells the baby it is all right to be low in the pecking order. I don't want competitive horses which lack attitude. I don't want a mare to teach a baby to fear humans, or run away when a handler approaches, or to kick or bite when being handled. What I want is a mare which will teach the foal all the ways to get along and enjoy the horse-human partnership. If the mare will do that, I'll wait to wean the baby.

When you decide to wean, plan ahead; be sure you are prepared.

There are two basic ways of weaning.

Dr. Alice likes to give both the mare and the foal a small amount of a tranquilizer before separation.

You can take the mare and foal to the barn, put the foal in a stall, and then return the mare to the pasture, or if you happen to have several mares and foals, you can remove a couple of dams, leaving the foals to play and seek solace with their companions.

Circumstances may dictate the method used, but in any case, the key element is to get the mare and foal separated by as great a distance as possible. If they can see each other or call to each other, the weaning is going to be much more traumatic and dangerous for both. When they can see or talk to each other, they will often attempt to get back together, even if it means going over, under or through fencing.

I like to prepare a stall for the mare and foal the night before weaning, then allow the foal to accept the stall while Momma is there. In the morning, I take the mare back to the pasture without Junior.

Check on the foal every hour or so to see he isn't getting too overheated, or cast or injured from bouncing around the stall.

Keep hay and grain in front of the foal at all times. The foal probably won't eat much, but even if he does, there is little danger it will hurt him.

Part of the planning should include a check on the water supply for the foal. If the barn has automatic waterers low enough, fine. If water buckets are used, they should not be left on the stall floor where they will be knocked over or become a source of injury.

Once the weaning is accomplished, Mamma isn't going to get her ration of grain, and I even cut back on her hay for a few days in an effort to help her milk dry up. It is also a good idea to limit the amount of water she is allowed. Three gallons every eight hours is about right. Check the mare's udder frequently. If it gets too tight and hot, rub gently with camphorated oil. Do not milk the mare as this prolongs the drying process, says Dr. Alice.

The cutback on the feed and water, plus the camphorated oil and the normal amount of exercise she'll take on her own, should be enough to avoid problems.

The checks on Mamma need not be as frequent as those on Baby, and usually it isn't necessary to spend much time reassuring her. Baby, however, may need three or four talk and groom sessions before he settles.

Just before bedtime, I like to check the mare, then the foal. You can give the foal a cube of sugar and tuck him in. If he cries and whines during the early part of the evening, be brave. Tomorrow he'll be all grown-up.

BE SMART, GELD

There are too many bad stallions around.

And too few good ones.

I'm not just talking about backyard stallions. I'm talking about a lot of bad stallions in the show ring, on the race track and at ranches.

And when I say bad, I'm not referring to disposition or manners. I'm referring to conformation and ability to perform.

Why, why, why do so many people insist on keeping so many poorly-conformed, poorly-bred, tangle-footed, jug-headed, slow pokes as stallions? I won't even mention all the ill-tempered, bad-mannered studs I've seen. I blame their behavior on their handlers, even though I know some of it is hereditary.

There are three good reasons to geld a horse.

1. Bad geldings don't perpetuate themselves, while bad stallions do, thereby lowering the quality of horses.

2. Geldings are normally easier to handle and have definitely savaged fewer handlers.

3. Good geldings are good for the horse business, while bad stallions are bad for business. Bad stallions produce horses of low quality, and therefore low price, and sometimes, due to low breeding fees, they keep some nice mares from going to some nice stallions.

Keeping a poorly-conformed, poorly-bred horse as a stallion guarantees only one thing: the majority of his offspring will be poorly-conformed and poorly-bred.

Usually, gelding a horse makes him easier to handle, easier to train and easier on himself. I've seen many a good stallion that would have been fantastic as a performance gelding if only his owner had had the good sense to help him.

As a stallion, the famous race horse, Kelso, was nothing. As a gelding, he was acclaimed horse of the century.

I've been told that a lot of would-be horsemen can't adjust psychologically to the idea of gelding a horse. I believe there's some truth to it. I've met quite a few psychotics in the horse business. I've yet to meet a real horseman who wouldn't say, "Cut that horse," when he could see it was best for the horse, the breed, the owner and the industry.

I have a feeling the same psychological problem holds true in a little different way for many women. I think a lot of would-be horsewomen idolize their tangle-footed, ill-conformed studs.

But then, a lot of women love bad men.

And some people never learn.

"A good gelding is always better than a bad stallion."
If there is a stallion in your herd, those words should be posted on the refrigerator door.

SO YOU'LL KNOW YOUR HORSE

I believe in music, love, friendship and that everything and everyone has an influence on everything and everyone. I believe we are all exactly right for the part we play in the universe and I believe the sun, the moon and the stars influence each of us, and our horses.

Once I wrote a series of articles entitled "The Zodiac Horse." The series touched off a major controversy. I was called everything from a prophet to a Satan worshipper.

I'm neither.

The opinions were nearly equally divided. Some said the material wasn't worth two cents. Others said it was the best understanding of their horses they had ever encountered.

For what it's worth, here's a quick synopsis of the 12 signs of the zodiac. Compare your horse's personality to his sign. If it is accurate, great; if not, it's still fun.

CAPRICORN--December 22 to January 19. This horse is always interested in the practical, organized, logical approach. He has a sense of his own worth, and his training must proceed along a well-planned path. A consistent teaching approach works well, while lavish praise or force will not work at all. The Capricorn horse is a natural "trail horse," being a born investigator.

AQUARIUS--January 20 to February 19. This horse is quick to learn anything, and in his natural field, be it jumping or reining, he'll seem to understand the challenges even before he has had formal schooling. The Aquarius horse loves independence and can't be stalled for days at a time.

He needs to be turned out frequently if he is to remain fresh and creative.

PISCES--February 20 to March 20. There are two sides to this horse's nature, and both are powerful. The Pisces horse does not normally make a good pleasure horse. He may be a brilliant mover, but he can't stand the mental boredom. Let him do work that challenges his talents. His fluid personality can't be forced into a rigid pattern.

ARIES--March 21 to April 20. This horse loves to take the lead. He is a natural race horse, endurance horse or three-day eventer. Because the Aries horse is self-assertive, his handler must be prepared to lock horns with him occasionally. The Aries horse is bold, sometimes difficult to handle.

TAURUS--April 21 to May 21. This horse will not be rushed into anything. He likes the status quo and is usually very content, but don't provoke him. He doesn't learn quickly because he doesn't like change. But teach him an exercise and he'll never forget it. He makes a very good show horse at almost any event.

GEMINI--May 22 to June 21. This horse is versatile, adaptable and inquisitive with a very changeable disposition. He is capable of learning a good deal, and he is usually very good at whatever it is you give him to do. But because he can master so much, he falls into his own trap--too much too soon.

CANCER--June 22 to July 23. This horse tends to yield, bend and flow around opposition. He is a master at passive resistance. You can't force him to learn or work. You have to plan ahead if you are going to be smarter than this horse. When handled correctly, you'll find this horse a super friend and willing worker. He's tough on the outside, but a big softy on the inside.

LEO--July 24 to August 23. The Leo horse is honest, inspired and truly gifted. Occasionally pompous and hard to train, he is also playful, loyal and lovable. The Leo horse is a natural show horse. He likes to shine. Of all horses, Leo horses need the most tender loving care and they perform in appreciation.

VIRGO--August 24 to September 23. For this horse, material comforts are extremely important. A good stall, good food and a good blanket are important. Treat him right and he'll treat you right. This horse will give his very best in every performance. However, because he is so willing to give, he expects the same from his rider. He is quick to anger if he knows more than his handler.

LIBRA--September 24 to October 23. This horse has a great sense of give and take. He makes an excellent Western horse because he can work on his own, and he makes a good English horse since he can compromise as well with his rider. Of all signs, Libra has the most versatility.

SCORPIO--October 24 to November 22. Very capable of showing explosive anger, this horse will kick, bite and strike. On the other hand, he is among the greatest performers. It is not unusual for the Scorpio horse to be more talented than the handler. If taken in the direction of his natural talents, the Scorpio is a sure champion. If taken in the wrong direction, he will be a flop. This horse is often saint or sinner.

SAGITTARIUS--November 23 to December 21. This horse is a natural athlete and must have plenty of work to remain healthy. He does best in events that are strenuous, such as jumping, racing or polo. Sagittarius horses hate to be bossed and will not succumb to force. Ask him nicely.

GUARDIAN ANGELS PROTECT

I know there are guardian angels.

If there weren't, there would be half as many horses and 80 per cent fewer horsemen.

"This horse has never made a bad move," she commented with a smile as she climbed aboard bareback and rode away using only a halter and lead rope.

Somewhere along the trail, the horse made a bad move. The X-rays showed only a tiny pelvic fracture. The soreness, they promised, would go away in a week or two.

"My daughter's horse never kicks," one mother told another.

The lawsuit is pending. The friend is mending. The horse hasn't kicked since.

"My horse loves me," she said, giving the horse a hug around the neck. "I know he'd never do anything to hurt me."

The cut above the eye will leave only a small scar. The one on the nose is doing just fine. She bought a new pair of sun glasses.

I can't believe it, but I see barefoot kids working around horses all the time. The other day, I watched a woman sit down on the grass not a foot away from her horse's hindquarters. Luckily, the horse only jumped sideways and the one hoof that did hit her only bruised her leg.

Why do we persist in this madness?

Because familiarity breeds contempt. We tend to be much less cautious around horses we know than those we don't. That seems to be human nature.

What we must do to reduce accidents is remain alert to the horse's nature, whether we know the horse or not.

The horse is a timid animal. He has difficulty in seeing things well, and he would sooner run than stay and investigate.

It is seldom that a horse will intentionally do anything to hurt you. The wreck nearly always happens as a result of the horse trying to get away from something he fears, whether the danger is real or imaginary. The injury results from the fact that the horse is enormously strong, weighs 1,000 pounds or more, doesn't reason too well and has very hard hoofs that are likely to be shod.

If he decides to occupy the same space I'm occupying, he usually does, since I'm skinny and don't move too fast.

In addition to accidents happening most frequently with the horses we know well, they are more likely to happen when we are performing routine tasks.

We tie a horse when we are going to groom him, saddle or unsaddle him, or go back to the tack room for something we forgot. We expect the horse to stand there quietly, and in most cases, he does. After a while, we become a little careless.

We start tying the horse by the reins, or we don't tie a slip knot, or we tie the horse to an object that is too low or too weak. Then the accident happens.

If we're lucky and don't get hurt, the horse usually does, and we say, "I never should have tied him there."

Carelessness in leading a horse is common. Even the best natured, best-trained horse should be led up next to you so you can see his head and ears. If the horse walks behind you at the end of the lead rope, it's more likely he'll jump on you, run over you or jerk you off your feet.

Everyone knows not to wrap a rope around your hand or arm or neck. But many still tempt fate.

Yes, it's the horses we know the best and love the most, the ones that would never hurt us, that do.

And that's why horsemen have guardian angels.

I sure hope they have a "no-strike" clause in their heavenly contract.

Breed Associations/Registries

Akhal-Teke Registry
Rt. 5, Box 110
Staunton, VA 24401

Andalusian, Lusitano
6020 Emerald Lane
Sykesville, MD 21784

American Assn. of
Owners, Breeders of
Peruvian Paso
PO Box 30723
Oakland, CA 94604

American Bashkir
Curly Registry
PO Box 246
Ely, NV 89301

American Buckskin
PO Box 3850
Redding, CA 96049

American Connemara
2360 Hunting Ridge Rd
Winchester, VA 22603

American Council of
Spotted Asses
PO Box 121
New Melle, MO 63365

American Cream
Draft Horse Assn.
2065 Noble Ave.
Charles City, IA 50616

Dartmoor Pony
15870 Pasco-Montra
Anna, OH 45302

American Dominant
Gray Registry
10980 "8" Mile Rd.
BattleCreek,
Michigan 49014

American Donkey
and Mule Society
2901 N. Elm
Denton, TX 76201

American Exmoor
Pony Registry
PO Box 477
Pittsboro, NC 27312

American Hackney
4059 Iron Works Rd.
Suite A
Lexington KY 40511

American
Hanoverian Society
4059 Iron Works Rd.
Suite C
Lexington KY 40511

American Indian
Horse Registry
Rt. 3, Box 64
Lockhart, TX 78644

Amer. Mammoth
Jackstock Registry
6513 W. Laurel Rd.
London, KY 40741

Amer. Miniature
Horse Association
5601 S. Interstate 35
Alvarado, TX 76009

Amer. Miniature
Horse Registry
6748 N. Frostwood
Peoria, IL 6161

American Morgan
Horse Assn.
PO Box 960
Shelburne, VT 05482

American Mustang
& Burro Registry
PO Box 788
Lincoln, CA 95648

American
Mustang Assn.
PO Box 338
Yucaipa, CA 92399

American Paint
Box 961023
Ft. Worth, TX 76161

Part-Blooded Horse
4120 S.E. River Dr.
Portland, OR 97267

Amer. Paso Fino
Assn., Inc.
PO Box 2363
Pittsburgh, PA 15230

American Quarter
Horse Association
PO Box 200
Amarillo, TX 79168

Quarter Pony Assn.
Box 30
NewSharon IA 50207

Amer. Saddlebred
Association
4093 Iron Works Pike
Lexington, KY 40511

Shetland Pony Club
6748 N. Frostwood
Peoria, IL 61615

Amer Shire Horse
35380 County Rd. 31
Davis, CA 95616

Amer. Suffolk Horse
4240 Goehring
Ledbetter, TX 78946

Amer. Trakehner
1520 W. Church St.
Newark, OH 43055

Amer. Warmblood
Registry, Inc.
PO Box 15167
Tallahassee, Fl 32317

Amer. Warmblood
6801 W. Romely
Phoenix, AZ 85043

Amer. Walera Pony
PO Box 401
Yucca Valley,
California 92286

American White &
Creme Registry
Rt. 1 Box 20
Naper, NE 68755

Appaloosa Horse
PO Box 8403
Moscow, ID 83843

Appaloosa Sport
Horse Assn.
1360 Saxonburg Blvd.
Glenshaw, PA 15116

Arabian Horse Reg.
of America
12000 Zuni St.
Westminster,
Colorado 80234

Arabian Sport Horse
6145 Whaleyville
Suffolk, VA 23438

Azteca Horse Reg.
PO Box 998
Ridgefield, WA 98642

Belgian Draft Horse
PO Box335
Wabash, IN 46992

Blazer Horse Assn.
820 N. Can-Ada Rd.
Star, ID 83669

Caspian Horse Soc.
9300 Hwy. 105
Brenham, TX 77833

Chickasaw Horse
169 Henry Martin Tr.
Love Valley NC 28677

Chilean Cornalero
5346 W. Sunnyside
Glendale, AZ 85304

Cleveland Bay Horse
PO Box 221
South Windham,
Connecticut, 06266

Clydesdale Breeders
17346 Kelley Rd.
Pecatonica, IL 61063

Colorado Ranger
RD 1, Box 1290
Wampum, PA 16157

Florida Cracker
PO Box 186
Newberry, FL 32669

**Foundation Quarter
Horse Association**
PO Box P
Joseph, OR 97846

Friesian Horse Assn
PO Box 11217
Lexington, Ky 40574

Galiceno Horse
PO Box 219
Godley, TX 76044

**Gliding Horse &
Pony Registration**
21055 Dog Bar Rd.
Grass Valley
California, 95949

Gotland Horse
PO Box 477
Pittsboro, NC 27312

**Haflinger Assn.
of America**
14570 Gratiot Rd.
Hemlock, MI 48626

Haflinger Registry
14640 State Rt. 83
Coshocton OH 43812

Half Quarter Horse
PO Box 931629
L.A., CA 90093

**Half Saddlebred
Registry of Amer.**
14640 State Rt. 83
Coshocton OH 43812

Hungarian Horse
HC 71, Box 108
Anselmo, NE 68813

Iberian Warmblood
122 Chapel Rd.
Middletown
Virgina. 22645

**Icelandic Horse
Adventure Society**
795 Entrance Rd.
Solvang, CA 93463

**Icelandic Horse
Trekkers**
PO Box 414937
Kansas City
Missouri, 64141

**Inter. Andalusian
Horse Association**
101 Carnoustie
Shoal Creek
Alabama 35242

**Inter. Arabian
Horse Association**
10805 E. Bethany Dr
Aurora, CO 80014

**Inter. Arabian
Horse Registry
Of North America**
12465 Brown-Moder
Marysville,OH43040

Inter. Bucksin
PO Box268
Shelby, IN 46377

**Inter. Colored
Appaloosa Assn.**
PO Box 99
Shipshewana,
Indiana 46565

Inter. Generic
PO Box 6778
Rancho Palos Verdes,
CA 90734

**Inter. Halter,
Pleasure Quarter
Horse Assn.**
11182 Hwy 69 N
Tyler, TX 75706

**Inter. Miniature
Donkey Registry**
1338 Hughes Shop
Westminster,
Maryland 21158

**Inter. Miniature
Trotting/Pacing**
780 Harney Rd.
LittlestownPA 17340

Morab Breeders
S. 101 W.
34628 Hwy. 99
Eagle, WI 53119

**Inter Plantation
Walking Horse**
PO Box 510
Haymarket VA22069

**Inter. Society for
Protection of
Mustangs/ Burros**
6212 E. Sweetwater
Scottsdale, AZ 85254

Inter. Sport Horse
939 Merchandise Mart
Chicago, IL 60654

Striped Horse Assn.
PO Box 209
Silver Cliff CO 81249

Trotting & Pacing
PO Box 751
Moravia, NY 13118

The Jockey Club
821 Corporate Dr.
Lexington, KY 40503

**Kentucky Mountain
Saddle Horse Assn.**
PO Box 505
Irvine, KY 40336

**KY Thoroughbred
Assn., Inc.**
PO Box 4040
Lexington, KY 40544

Kiger Mesteno Assn.
Box 1200
Pinedale, WY 82941

**Lipizzan Association
of North America**
PO Box 1133
Anderson , IN 46015

**Missouri Fox
Trotting Horse Assn.**
PO Box 1027
Ava, MO 65608

Montana Travler
Box 1376
Livingston, MT 59047

Mountain Pleasure
PO Box 670
Paris, KY 40361

**National Grade
Horse Assn.**
2459 Tualatin Valley
Hillsboro, OR 97123

**National Barrel
Horse Assn.**
PO Box 1377
Hanford, CA 93232

**National
Chincoteague Pony**
2595 Jensen Rd.
BellinghamWA98226

**National Cutting
Horse Assn.**
4704 Hwy 377 S.
Ft. Worth, TX 76116

**Half-Tennessee
Walking Horse Reg.**
PO Box 160
Herald, CA 95638

**National Pinto
Horse Reg.**
PO Box 486
Oxford, NY 13830

**National Quarter
Pony Assn.**
PO Box 216
Baltimore, OH 43105

**National Reined
Cow Horse**
1318 Jepsen
Corcoran, CA 93212

National Reining
Horse Association
448 Main St.
Suite 204
Coshocton, OH 43143

National Show
Horse Registry
11700 Commonwealth
Suite 200
Louisville, KY 40299

National Spotted
Saddle Horse
PO Box 898
Murfreesboro,
Tennesee 37130

New Forest Pony
PO Box 206
Pascoag, RI 02859

N.A. Corriente Assn.
PO Box 12359
N. Kansas City,
Missouri 64116

North American
Exmoors
RR 4, Box 273
Amherst Nova Scotia
B4H 3Y2
Canada

Mustang Assn. & Reg
PO Box 850906
Mesquite, TX 75185

N.A. Saddle Mule
Association
Box 1574
Boyd, TX 76023

Selle Francais Horse
PO Box 646
Winchester, VA 22604

N.A. Singlefooting
Association
PO Box 1079
Three Forks MT59751

N.A. Trakehner Assn.
PO Box 12172
Lexington, KY 40581

N.A. Warmblood
2400 Faussett Rd.
Howell, MI 48843

Norwegian Fjord
Assn
24570 N. Chardon
Rd.
Grayslake, IL 60030

Ohio Quarter
Horse Association
101 Tawa Rd.
Richwood OH 43444

Palomino Horse
Breeders of
America
15253 E. Skelly Dr.
Tulsa, OK 74116

Part Thoroughbred
Remount Assn.
PO Box 1901
Middleburg, VA
22117

Paso Fino Horse
101 N. Collins St.
Plant City, FL 33566

Percheron Horse
Assn
Box 141
Fredericktown,
Ohio 43019

Peruvian Paso
Horse
3077 Wiljan Ct.
Suite A
Santa Rosa, CA
95407

Pintabian Horse
PO Box 360
Karlstad, MN 56732

Pinto Horse Assn.
of America, Inc.
1900 Samuels Ave.
Ft. Worth, TX 76102

Pony of Americas
5240 Elmwood Ave.
IndianapolisIN46203

Purebred
Hanoverian Assn.
PO Box 429
Rocky Hill, NJ08553

Racking Horse Assn
67 Horse Center Rd.
Decatur, AL 35603

Rare Color Morgan
RR 3 Box 353
Emlenton, PA 16373

Society for
Preservation of
the Barb Horse
3900 N. Crane Rd.
Midvale, ID 83645

Southwest
Spanish Mustang
HCR 3, Box 7670
Wilcox, AZ 85643

Spanish-Barb Assn.
PO Box 598
Anthony, FL 32617

Spanish-Norman
Horse Registry
PO Box 985
Woodbury, CT 06798

Spotted Saddle
Horse Exhibitors
PO Box 1046
Shelbyville TN 37160

Steens Mountain
Kiger Registry
26450 Horsell
Bend, OR 97701

Swedish Warmblood
PO Box 1587
Coupeville, WA98239

Tennessee Walking
Horse Breeders
PO Box 286
Lewisburg, TN 37091

Texas Corriente
PO Box 55
Wortham, TX 76693

Tiger Horse Assn.
1445 Dry Fork Rd.
Granville, TN 38564

United Quarab Reg.
31100 Fernwood Rd.
Newberg, OR 97132

U.S. Cavalry
Association
PO Box 2325
Ft. Riley, KS 66442

U.S. Icelandic
Horse Congress
38 Park St.
Montclair, NJ 07042

U.S. Lipizzan
Registry
707 13th St. S.E.
Suite 275
Salem, OR 97301

US Trotting Assn.
750 Michigan Ave.
Columbus, OH 43215

Walkaloosa Horse
3815 N. Cambell Rd.
Otis Orchards,
Washington 99027

Welsh Pony
& Cob Society
PO Box 2977
Winchester, VA 22604

Westfalen
Warmblood Assn.
18432 Biladeau Lane
Penn Valley, CA95946

Index